THE ACADEMIC CORPORATION

ALLEN FENICHEL & DAVID MANDEL

THE ACADEMIC CORPORATION

Justice, Freedom, and the University

Introduction by Professor J.C. Weldon

Montréal-New York

Copyright 1987 ©
Black Rose Books Inc.

No part of this book may be reproduced or transmitted in any form by means, electronic or mechanical, including photocopying and recording, or by any information storage or retrieval system, without written permission from the publisher, except for brief passages quoted by a reviewer in a newspaper or magazine.

Black Rose Books No. P 112

Canadian Cataloguing in Publication Data

Fenichel, Allen, 1936-
    The academic corporation

ISBN 0-920057-96-9 (bound). — ISBN 0-920057-97-7 (pbk.).

1. Academic freedom. 2. Academic freedom—Québec (Province)—Montréal—Case studies. I. Mandel, David, 1947- II. Title.

LB2332.M35 1987   378'.121   C87-090041-2

Cover design: Jennifer DeFreitas

Black Rose Books

3981 boul. St. Laurent   340 Nagel Dr.
Montréal, Qué. H2W 1Y5   Cheektowaga, N.Y. 14225
Canada   USA

Printed and bound in Québec, Canada

This book is dedicated to the memory of Jack Weldon, who died in February 1987 at the age of sixty-four.

On November 24, 1978, the McGill Senate, with only one dissenting voice, censured Professors J.C. Weldon and A. Asimakopulos, both distinguished McGill professors of long standing and members of the Royal Society of Canada. The events leading up to this decision began with a letter dated January 16, 1978, to the then dean of arts, Robert Vogel, from an associate professor in the Economics Department requesting that normal procedure be bypassed in the decision on his promotion to full professor: he asked that his case be considered not by the Economics Department's promotion committee but by a university committee. He claimed that Professors Weldon and Asimakopulos were prejudiced against him.

A recent report by the Canadian Association of University Teachers (*CAUT Bulletin*, May 1987) found that in his efforts on behalf of "Professor X," Dean Vogel misled the Senate in asking it to set in motion the establishment of a Statutory Selection

Committee for promotion to full professor without a department recommendation on this matter. It also established that the Senate Committee on Disclosure of Information, which was asked to investigate the circulation of documents by Weldon and Asimakopulos (an attempt on their part to show that the Senate had been misled), acted precipitously, ignored due process, and knowingly exceeded its mandate when it condemned them. The findings of this committee provided the basis for the Senate's censure of the two professors. The Senate, in turn, compounded the committee's error by also acting precipitously and without regard for due process. Further, it was found to be an inappropriate body to make such judgements. The CAUT Report accused the university administration, particularly Principal Bell, and the Senate, of recklessly damaging the reputation of two outstanding academics.

The McGill administration was also found to be responsible for blocking a resolution of the grievance. CAUT concluded that not only are the existing grievance procedures at McGill seriously flawed, but that the administration, and specifically Principal Johnston, who succeeded Bell, have refused either to provide the necessary leadership to repair the flaws or to make available reasonable alternative procedures.

Despite this report, Weldon and Asimakopulos remain condemned at McGill. Despite the nine years spent in pursuit of justice, justice has eluded them. In all those years, not one member of the Senate that censured them has come forward to admit error, or even to pose suitable questions. The vast majority of the faculty have ignored the issue. Even sympathetic colleagues often seem unable to comprehend why Jack would give so much of himself to what appears to them a relatively insignificant matter.

Yet in the final version of his curriculum vitae, Jack described this struggle as the most important contribution of his academic career. He explains in his introduction to this book:

> There is only one "Dreyfus" case, it seems to me, one only, played over and over again to audiences of every variety and size, and picturing victories and defeats that are never final and never complete. For civilized people, attendance

at the play is mandatory and soon demands participation upon the stage from the audience itself.

For Jack Weldon, these were not empty words. He lived by that philosophy. Even when, as in his own grievance, the cost was high and the results uncertain, he could not ignore injustice. The tragedy of cases like those of Weldon-Asimakopulos and Mandel lies not in any excess on the part of the offended, but rather in the failure of their colleagues, despite their claimed professional commitment to the pursuit of truth, to seek out that truth and uphold it in the face of corrupt authority.

If one were to apply Jack's criterion in judging the fate of these grievances, one would have to conclude that our universities count few civilized people among their staffs today. In these cases, CAUT, which purports to represent all of Canada's university teachers, has behaved little better than members of the "McGill community." (It required nine years and untold efforts to obtain the Weldon-Asimakopulos report, which itself is not a formal censure of McGill.) For if injustice can exist in the Canadian academic setting, this is not—as it is in some societies—because of the overwhelming pressures of a "totalitarian" state. Rather, it is because of the timidity of academics, timidity nourished by corporatist narrowness and egotism.

Jack Weldon showed those of us who were fortunate enough to work and struggle alongside him the difference even one civilized person, one man of principle and courage, can make.

Table of Contents

Acknowledgements 13
Preface 15
Chronology 17
Cast of Characters 19
Introduction by Professor J.C. Weldon 23

1 **The Decision-Making Process** 31
   The Decision: No Discussion, No Explanation, No
      Appeal 34
   The Academic Setting: Associations, Unions,
      Collegia 42

2 **Obtaining a Hearing** 47

3 **The Hearings** 61
   Setting the Stage 62
   The University Resists 66
   Testimony 76

4	**The Reports**	95
	Canadianization	95
	Procedural Defects	98
	Political Bias	103
	Remedy	109
5	**Implementing the Gibson Report: Three Strikes and You're Out**	111
	The First Blow	111
	The Second Blow	117
	The Third Blow	126
	Not With a Bang, But With a Whimper	131
	Postscript	135

Conclusion: Academic Freedom and Accountability 139

Appendix I: Gibson Committee Proposals Concerning Fair Appointment Practices in Canadian Universities 153

Appendix II: Canadian Association of University Teachers' Guidelines on Canadianization and the University 159

Acknowledgements

In writing this book we have many debts to acknowledge—to those who aided and supported us in pursuing the grievance and to others who helped in the preparation of the manuscript. In particular, we want to thank A. Asimakopulos, Michael Barnwell, Jane Broderick, Adrienne Chinn, Armand Côté, Bronna Fenichel, E.S. Goodden, Terry Goodden, Sid Ingerman, Andrea Levy, Sonia Mandel, Pauline Vaillancourt, and many others who lent us their support. Finally, there are those we would thank but who are better served by going unnamed.

Preface

On April 29, 1980, the Political Science Department at McGill University voted to deny David Mandel a teaching position. This would normally have been the end of the matter. Universities do not accept the right of society to question their decisions, and, on new appointments, even otherwise limited but available self-monitoring arrangements are largely non-operative. Terms such as "academic freedom" and "global judgement" are put forward to protect universities from public scrutiny. David Mandel's situation was different because he expected, and soon came to demand, an explanation for the department's decision. It did not take long for him to realize that he would get no such explanation, and that, in fact, McGill University would resist any effort on his part to obtain an impartial hearing.

This book is the story of David Mandel's efforts to obtain a hearing—a hearing which, when realized, upheld his allegations of wrongdoing yet gave him no redress. It also deals with the nature and results of that hearing and the broader issues they raise. We have tried to let the various participants speak for themselves through their correspondence, testimony, and reports.

The four years the case lasted yielded an overwhelming amount of written material.

David Mandel's experience with McGill University, the Canadian Association of University Teachers (CAUT), the Québec Human Rights Commission, and the provincial and federal immigration authorities raises troubling questions about justice and accountability in our university system. It also poses questions about the role of "academic freedom." While most people assume that the principle exists to safeguard the autonomy of academics in their pursuit of knowledge, few are aware of its ideological uses as a screen to shield from outside scrutiny the subversion of the very freedom it proclaims and to prevent the appeal of unjust decisions. This case also casts grave doubt on the government's and CAUT's commitment to their own laws and guidelines designed to promote the "Canadianization" of our universities, by affording priority in hiring to qualified Canadians.

Our purpose in writing this book is to draw the attention of the academic community and the public to these issues as well as to dispel some widespread and harmful illusions about universities and their place in society.

Chronology

Aug. 1979 Mandel appointed visiting professor of Soviet and East European politics in the Department of Political Science, McGill University

Mar. 1980 McGill advertises tenure-track post in Soviet and East European politics

Apr. 1980 Appointments Committee of the Political Science Department chooses Mandel as the most qualified applicant by a vote of 5 v. 3

Apr. 1980 Departmental meeting votes 13 v. 9 and 1 abstention to reject Appointment Committee's recommendation

Mar. 1981 CAUT Board decides to set up its own fact-finding committee to proceed without McGill's cooperation after the university refuses to participate in a joint inquiry and the Academic Freedom and Tenure Committee drops its call for an investigation

Oct. 1981 CAUT Board's fact-finding committee arrives at McGill and conducts its inquiry

Oct. 1981- *Sept. 1982*	Human Rights Commission hearing
Oct. 1982	CAUT fact-finding committee final report
Nov. 1982	Human Rights Commission receives report of Mandel inquiry that finds political discrimination but reverses this decision
Mar. 1983	CAUT Board resolves that the evidence raises "grave doubts" as to whether Mandel was treated fairly; it decides to once again ask McGill to participate in a joint inquiry and, failing that, that a subcommittee present the next Board meeting with a "summary and analysis" of the case, with a view to publication
July 1983	Principal Johnston refuses third CAUT request for joint inquiry
Nov. 1983	CAUT Board agrees to publish article with findings of committee, views of Board, and statement of general concerns raised by case
Apr. 1984	*CAUT Bulletin* publishes full report of fact-finding committee, alongside negative "report" of Academic Freedom and Tenure Committee

Cast of Characters

David Mandel, candidate for the position in Soviet and East European politics in McGill's Political Science Department

Allen Fenichel, associate professor in McGill's Economics Department and Mandel's academic adviser in his dispute with the university

McGill's Political Science Department, 1979-80

Appointments Committee
   Professors

   Frank Kunz, chair
   Jerome Black
   Stephen Bornstein
   Barbara Haskel
   James R. Mallory
   James Tulley

Students

David Harris
Andrey Hollinger

Additional department members

Professors

Michael Brecher
Thomas Bruneau
Daniel Latouche
Baldev Nayar
Paul Noble
Samuel Noumoff
Filippo Sabetti

Richard Schultz
John Shingler
Janice Stein
Blema Steinberg
Charles Taylor
Dale Thomson
Harold Waller

Students

Jean Contratti
Anita Isaacs
Gérald Lévesque
P. Ramasamy

McGill's Administration

(Professors)

David Johnston (Law), Principal, 1979-present

Eigel Pedersen (Education), Vice-Principal Academic, 1971-81

Samuel Freedman (Medicine), Vice-Principal Academic, 1981-present

Robert Vogel (History), Dean of Arts, 1971-81

Michael Maxwell (History), Dean of Arts, 1981-86

McGill's Association of University Teachers (MAUT)

(Professors)

John Harrod (Chemistry), President, 1981-82
Jagdish Handa (Economics), President, 1982-83
Irving Gopnik (English), Chair, Grievance Committee

Canadian Association of University Teachers (CAUT)

Victor Sim, Executive Secretary

Prof. Kenneth McGovern (Philosophy, University of Regina), President, 1982-83

Prof. Sarah Shorten (Philosophy, University of Western Ontario), President, 1983-85

Academic Freedom and Tenure Committee (AF&T)

(Professors)

James Foulks (Pharmacology, University of British Columbia), Chair, 1978-81

Jill Vickers (Political Science, Carleton University), Chair, Jan.-March 1981

James Hiller (History, Memorial University), Chair, 1981-85

Fact-Finding Committee—David Mandel Inquiry

(Professors)

Dale Gibson (Law, University of Manitoba), Chair
André Côté (Philosophy, Laval University)
Keith Johnstone (English, University of Saskatchewan)

Québec Human Rights Commission (HRC)

Francine Fournier, Chair
Claude Trudel, Investigator, Mandel Inquiry

Additional Participants

Jules O. Duchesneau, McGill's lawyer

René Martel, lawyer for Fédération des associations des professeurs des universités du Québec (FAPUQ)

Prof. J. C. Weldon, Economics, McGill University

Prof. Fred C. Engelmann, University of Alberta, President (1985), Canadian Political Science Association

Gretta Chambers, Member, McGill's Board of Governors

21

Joan Debardeleben, successful applicant for the position in Soviet and East European politics in McGill's Political Science Department

David Wootton, visiting professor in the Political Science Department, 1981-83

Pauline Vaillancourt, assistant professor in the Political Science Department, 1969-72

Introduction

In 1979 David Mandel was a young scholar who had just been given a visiting appointment for the year ahead in McGill's Department of Political Science. During his term, a regular assistant professorship became available to the department. The new position was advertised in a routine way. Mandel submitted an application. The department soon engaged itself in compiling a short list of candidates.

Eventually, the Appointments Committee designated Mandel as its "preferred candidate." He was also the only Canadian to have been short-listed. Thus, if some other applicant were to be chosen, that other person could not be a Canadian; but then, because of the laws governing jobs and immigration, a non-Canadian could be appointed only if Mandel's suitability were denied: on the face of things Mandel's application would have to be successful. All the same, that application failed, and out of the causes and effects of its failure came the series of surprising and depressing events Fenichel and Mandel have chronicled.

Perhaps the history is best read as a morality play, familiar enough in its classical themes but novel and even frightening in its details. Rights and wrongs are to be found in abundance, but these rights and wrongs are not at all evenly distributed amongst the players. Mandel was rejected, so this review and its sources tell us, because *some* members of the Department of Political Science had been greatly offended by his political attitudes and activities, and by their hostility they induced *several more* members of this society to be expedient and defer to the wishes of their offended colleagues. The more senior of this acquiescent group chose to express collegial solidarity with their offended colleagues, and the more junior, prudent judgement about how their own futures might unfold. Political considerations should not intrude upon academic judgements, true—a proposition on which all professed to agree—but that abstract guide to conduct could be set aside by reasonable people when the cost was, after all, nothing more harmful than a small interruption in the career of a young visitor. Reasonable people could charge even that cost to the intransigence of their less enlightened friends, and count it a cost that would be easily redeemed within the comforting calm of a harmonious future.

Little is more appalling in the narrative than how easily the acquiescent closed their eyes, pretended Mandel's shattered career was an everyday accident of academic life, and treated a flat contradiction of academic law as contributing to integrity and stability for the long run. This, of course, is by no means an assessment made at arm's length. I have long known Fenichel, came to know Mandel well in the months following his dismissal, and from "pre-Mandel" to now have been engaged in a quarrel of my own about administrative lawlessness.

Some of the history I became acquainted with at first hand. All of it seems to be well supported by Fenichel and Mandel's primary sources. The authors will in any case speak for themselves in the pages that follow, and the interested and careful amongst their readers will want to test all indictments against other accounts of the evidence. Still, it is comforting in preparing this Introduction to see how closely its impressions are duplicated by the only extensive, direct investigations that outside reviewers have made. Those investigations were two, the study made on behalf of the

Québec Human Rights Commission and that made on behalf of the Canadian Association of University Teachers. Perhaps it is fair to add an investigation that was asked for but denied, the joint inquiry the authorities at McGill were repeatedly invited to assist, but whose purposes they declined to recognize. Silence speaks loudly and frequently at McGill, where the requirement of review by "peers" is routinely condemned in principle when it touches administrative authority, so that it may safely be ignored in practice.

Someone not unfriendly once remarked that partisans in such a cause must beware of disproportion, must not see Dreyfus in every parochial injustice. It is, I think, a doubly interesting misconception. The importance of "Dreyfus" was not that high authority of a great power would betray justice for reasons of state, but that *any* authority of *any* institution could claim justification for a betrayal of trust motivated by reasons that would separate a "state" from its laws and functions. There *is* no vast difference of scale. The betrayal on either side of the comparison is *commonplace*, repeatedly experienced both in small domains and in large. What is more, it is essentially the same betrayal in all its particular appearances. There is one "Dreyfus" case, it seems to me, one only, played over and over again to audiences of every variety and size, and picturing victories and defeats that are never final and never complete. For civilized people, attendance at the play is mandatory and soon demands participation upon the stage from the audience itself.

And at the Royal Institution for the Advancement of Learning, who behaved badly and who behaved well in *this* particular performance? It often happens in these dramas that some brief episode captures, if not everything, then a great deal. One picks an exchange that took place in the investigation before the Human Rights Commission. Here is the vice-principal (academic) of McGill confronted by Fenichel with a signed report that shows testimony he has just given is false. Freedman does not plead mistaken memory or respond in embarrassment, but displays annoyance at this challenge to authority and the failure of his officials to control information. The guardian-in-chief of our academic protocol demands to know of his tormentor "how this confidential document came into [your] possession." Shown his blunder (one will stipulate the softest interpretation), the vice-principal had an obvious duty to repair the damage his testimony had done to Mandel. He gives his allegiance instead to a subtler duty under which a Mandel would count for very little. Fenichel has exposed a truth that a loyalist should have kept hidden. He, and not Freedman, has forgotten how a true son of McGill should behave.

One is tempted to give equal billing to the correspondence from the ineffable Michael Maxwell. The exchanges with Gibson of the Association of University Teachers will entrance any reader who collects examples of pompous folly. What a curious view it is that a university is a community capable of being a state within the state, a community in which open inquiry is best carried out in darkness! Buffoonery, though, colours rather than inspires these events. Far more important is the shabbiness of the proceedings in the Department of Political Science, the disregard in a real situation of everything taught about lawfulness for hypothetical situations. I doubt that any of the participants had much trouble in rationalizing his or her role in what had taken place, that any found it necessary to calculate or conspire rather than surrender to reflexive decisions. The deeds were savage in their effects, but they were drab and petty in their origins.

As with the department, so with the administrative apparatus of the greater university, so with the staff association (the McGill Association of University Teachers), and so with every institution at McGill that became involved with the affair: one must not disturb the community lest it be hindered by small truths *now* from its mission to search out large truths in a golden age to come.

It is correctly said, I suppose, that the university is the depository to which great freedoms have been entrusted, freedoms of inquiry, of opinion, of expression, of dissent. It might seem to follow that the university is therefore not only custodian but sworn defender of that immense trust. Alas, so far as one might generalize from Mandel and McGill, we have encountered a non-sequitur. The hypothesis has to be entertained that full-blown monsters (regimes and personalities in the mould of Hitlerian Germany or Stalinist Russia) may quite correctly decide that greater resistance can be expected from gypsies or Jehovah Witnesses than from all the academics of a realm. There may be a noble creed on the campus but not a creed that has actual adherents or real defenders, a trust accepted and daily proclaimed but not a trust around which the nominal trustees are found to rally.

The reader will find still stronger evidence than that supplied "on campus" in the weakness and vacillation displayed by the Canadian Association of University Teachers. Imagine an organization that backs away from the findings of its own investigators, begs the institution that its investigators have condemned to join in still one further inquiry (though McGill has refused at all times to permit outside review); imagine such an organization, on being rebuffed, sacrificing its client entirely rather than show incivility to his oppressors. The association doffed its cap, politely tugged at its forelock, and apologized to authority for the nuisance it had created: and so in this manner did it demonstrate the vigour young academics could expect from their protector.

Little better can be said of the Québec Human Rights Commission, which also preferred to live to fight another day (those other days of battle and duty that never dawn!) rather than stand behind Mandel, its own investigator, its own investigation. Agencies with a mandate to protect their clients and the public choose instead to protect themselves.

There is, however, another side to this bleak story. One does not know how representative McGill is. Its curious pattern of government, its detachment from the society around it, may make it eccentric even in its sins. (As taxpayers we hand over to a self-appointing and unrepresentative body of "governers" scores of millions of dollars to be spent each year according to whatever mixture of wisdom and whim occupies their minds, not a process easily reconciled with textbooks about responsible government.) Reports in the *Bulletin* of the Canadian Association of University Teachers show that other universities also behave badly, but they also contain news of administrations that have behaved well: much seems to turn on the moral direction given or denied by the leading figures in the bureaucracy of a university. More consequentially, in each of the institutions on which I have commented there have been persons, or even subordinate institutions, from whom protest flowed (at times protest that called for courage as well as principle), or who have been derelict in *this* situation but responsible in some other.

Mandel himself provides fresh air in this suffocating atmosphere. He is a quiet, understated person, likely to strike one as an easy victim rather than a determined defender of law. He most certainly should have been left alone, for he has fought back with dignity, skill, and immense endurance, forcing one group after another to choose between assistance to justice or complicity with injustice. It is *still* an open question as to whether those who have sold themselves in this business—surely the Devil has been a spendthrift in a market where the cheapest title has proved payment-enough—will find themselves better remembered for their roles in the "Mandel" case than for any of the scholarly work they will have published as comfortable truth. In that respect, the contest is far from over.

Gibson and his colleagues (the investigators for the association) compel respect. Jon Thompson should be similarly mentioned were he not closer to my own "grievance" than to Mandel's, so let the mention all the same be made. Were our freedoms always protected by such as these they would be freedoms well protected indeed. Trudel acted as investigator for the Human Rights Commission with similar distinction. One speaks only briefly of these persons who performed their duties, but one would not wish that brevity be taken for *casual* respect. This company of the non-expedient contains an admirable membership.

Let me close with a few words to those who pay the bills for the universities. You are bound to conclude from Fenichel and Mandel that Canadian universities are now separated from accountability. What is mythical about their pretensions and what is real? You may or may not draw the same conclusions about the "Mandel" case that some of us from McGill have drawn. My chief hope is that McGill is not typical, my corresponding fear is that except in degree it probably *is* typical, and my concern is how academics and the public-at-large can rescue their universities from institutional settings that may guarantee corruption.

You should at the least, I think, be alarmed at the possibility of great abuse and great waste being hidden within these universities that are both autocratically governed and the final judges of their own behaviour. Institutions that preach freedom but practise secrecy are not citizens above reproach, nor are their deeds automatically above suspicion. You know practically nothing about McGill that its authorities prefer be hidden from you, for you have allowed it to become a closed community, self-serving and irresponsible. Fenichel and Mandel may succeed in persuading you how unhealthy the situation has become, how contradictory of openness and tolerance for dissent, how subversive of the true university. They may also persuade you that phantom organizations for *defending* freedoms *endanger* freedoms more than most examples of open abuse.

J. C. Weldon
Professor of Economics

1 The Decision-Making Process

David Mandel was born in Toronto in 1947 to Polish-Jewish immigrants. His father started out as a worker in the fur industry but spent the main part of his working life in a small family dairy his own father had established on Baldwin Street, in what was once the heart of Toronto's Jewish immigrant district. In the latter part of his life he was involved in real estate.

Mandel attended a Hebrew day school, graduating in 1965 with several awards, including one for the highest grades in the provincial senior matriculation exams in French and Russian. It was at this school, as well as in the religious labour-Zionist youth movement, that his socialist world view first took form. A particular influence were the writings of the Hebrew prophets, taught at the school by a man who had participated in the Russian civil war on the side of the Bolsheviks and who was himself the disowned son of a famous Lithuanian rabbi.

Upon graduation, Mandel went to Israel to work on a kibbutz and eventually enrolled in the Hebrew University in the Departments of Russian Studies and French Civilization. He supported himself working as an assistant in the Russian Language Department and spent his summers and holidays working on a kibbutz and in construction. It was at the Hebrew University, in a course on Old Church Slavonic, that he met his future wife, a Lithuanian immigrant whose family had left the Soviet Union in 1959.

In 1969, with a Bachelor of Arts degree, he left for Columbia University in New York, where he had been granted a four-year faculty fellowship and admission to the Department of Sociology and the Russian Institute. A year later, his daughter Ruthy was born. Mandel supplemented his fellowship income by working as a teaching assistant and as a truck driver. He also spent a year as a labourer in a New Jersey iron foundry.

At the time of Mandel's arrival, Columbia was in the midst of anti-war ferment, and it was during his participation in these anti-war activities, as well as in the student movement (the Graduate Sociology Student Union, in particular, was a centre of radical activism) that his hitherto vague socialist outlook took on a firmly Marxist form. These views led him to his doctoral thesis topic: a study of the consciousness and role of the workers of Petrograd in the Russian Revolution. In the course of his work on the thesis, Mandel received a Canada-USSR Exchange scholarship which allowed him and his family to spend a year in Leningrad. There he pursued archival and library research and worked part-time for a Soviet publishing company.

Mandel's thesis challenged the then prevailing views on the Russian Revolution. He showed that the workers were the moving force in the revolution and that their support for the Bolsheviks, themselves in the majority workers, was a conscious choice. Indeed, the Bolsheviks' strongest support came from the more skilled and politically literate working-class elements, especially the metalworkers.

The political implications of this thesis, or possibly Mandel's own politics in the Sociology Department at Columbia—or more likely, a combination of the two—did not please the two sociologists on his dissertation committee, who attempted to impose "major revisions" on the work. As it stood, they argued, it was not sufficiently "scientific." Neither of these sociologists were Russian experts. The other three people on the committee, however—a historian, an economist, and a political scientist, all well-known authorities in Russian and Soviet Studies—insisted that the dissertation was original and excellent and refused the demand for "major revisions," a demand which was tantamount to failing it since the required revisions would have been unacceptable to Mandel.

The debate following the defence raged on for some two hours behind closed doors (ordinarily, such a discussion would last about twenty minutes), but the Russian experts were in a majority and refused to concede. A compromise was finally reached: the thesis would pass but Mandel would have to revise its conclusion, a critique of sociological theories of revolution. His thesis supervisor, a man with whom he had worked for four years and who had never given him a hint that there was anything wrong with the thesis, now advised him to leave sociology, because "you can be critical but not negative." (Mandel's grades in the Sociology Department had been consistently excellent.) After the defence, one of the sociologists complained to the dean about the foul language used by a certain professor at the defence. One of the Russian specialists, it seems, had called him a "son of a bitch." Columbia's Russian Institute did not share the sociologists' negative assessment; they granted Mandel a post-doctoral fellowship to enable him to expand his thesis in preparation for publication.

At the end of his fellowship, Mandel was appointed to a one-year visiting position in the Department of Political Science and the Centre for Russian and East European Studies (CREES) at the University of Birmingham in England. His experience at CREES, a major centre of its kind in the West, was a positive one. Despite the broad range of political views among the staff, ranging from Marxist to conservative, there was a genuinely shared commitment to the field that made for an intellectually open and stimulating atmosphere. Indeed, after the year at Birmingham, Mandel was disposed to see Columbia's Sociology Department as a sad exception, a view that left him quite unprepared for the Political Science Department at McGill.

In the spring of 1979, Mandel applied for a one-year post at McGill University in Soviet and East European politics that he had seen advertised in *University Affairs*. This job was especially attractive in that it would allow him not only to return to Canada (and there were indications that a permanent position might become available) but also to live in Québec and finally put his French to use. A few weeks later, he was interviewed at Oxford by three McGill political scientists, who recommended to the department that he be hired.

The Decision: No Discussion, No Explanation, No Appeal

In March 1980, after Mandel had been at McGill for about six months, the department advertised a three-year assistant professorship, stating that "candidates are expected to teach courses in the area of Soviet and East European Politics, comparative Communism, Soviet Marxism and Soviet foreign policy," the areas in which Mandel had been teaching at McGill and Birmingham. The only other requirements in the notice were facility in Russian and a "completed Ph.D. degree," both of which Mandel possessed.

Mandel applied, thinking his chances were good. The students appreciated him as a teacher (all five student delegates at the departmental meeting would vote in favour of his appointment), and he had just signed a contract with Macmillan Press in England to publish an expanded version, in two volumes, of his study of the Russian Revolution. He became even more hopeful in mid-April when he was told that the Appointments Committee (consisting of five professors and three students) had chosen him from among some two dozen applicants as the most qualified for the post.

There were, however, some worrying signs. The vote in the Appointments Committee had been five against three. Professor Stephen Bornstein, a friend of Mandel in the committee, had spoken to him of the strong opposition to his candidacy on the part of at least two of its members. The basis of this opposition was strangely vague and fluid. It seemed, as a student member of the committee later testified, that "they wanted anyone but Mandel." At one point, according to Bornstein's later testimony, Professor Frank Kunz, the chair of the department, told him, without offering any further comment, that there was a group of professors strongly opposed to Mandel. In the two weeks separating the Appointments Committee's decision and the departmental meeting, Mandel received reports from students and professors of intense lobbying efforts on the part of those opposed to him.

It did not take much imagination to guess the sources of this opposition. As Professor Sam Noumoff put it some months later in a letter to *The McGill Daily*:

1. Dr. Mandel is a Marxist in a department where this view is not shared by many.
2. Dr. Mandel does not share the views held by some on the central problems of the Middle East.
3. Dr. Mandel associated himself with the McGill Faculty Union and its support of the maintenance strike, in which he joined a small minority in the department.

It would be naive to believe that one or more of the[se] factors did not play some role in the outcome.

Noumoff's cryptic statement requires some elaboration. As a Marxist, Mandel makes clear in his teaching and his politics his opposition to a system in which vast wealth is wielded by a few in the pursuit of profit at the expense of the many. As a political scientist, he rejects the dominant view of a liberal state as a neutral arbiter among basically equal competing interests. While not denying a certain reality to the democratic structures, he insists on the limits to democracy imposed by the concentration of economic power and by the very logic of the capitalist economy, whose health, measured by the return on capital, is the state's foremost concern—next, that is, to defending The True North Strong and Free from the red hordes massed beyond the polar cap. This latter function is fulfilled principally by a policy of blind solidarity with U.S. imperial interests.

Mandel considers the Soviet Union, about which he principally taught at McGill, neither capitalist nor socialist. Its planned (or, rather, administered) economy is managed by a conservative party-state bureaucracy bent on maintaining its absolute sway over society. But this society is not the monolithic grouping of atomized individuals portrayed by the theorists of totalitarianism. Soviet workers, despite their having been politically expropriated, enjoy certain social rights unknown under capitalism, in particular the right to employment. Indeed, the chronic labour shortage affords them a degree of shopfloor power that acts indirectly as an important restraint on the regime.

In teaching about the Soviet Union, Mandel is careful that his criticism not be taken as support or justification for our own system, with its different but nevertheless real kind of oppression. His point of departure in both cases is the interests of the working class, those at the bottom of the hierarchies of power and privilege who must live from the sale of their labour. One of Mandel's students at McGill, herself far from radically inclined, put it this way in a letter of support for Mandel to the Canadian Association of University Teachers (CAUT) dated June 19, 1980: "Professor Mandel has a deep-set love of ordinary people that emanates from his research and teaching and from his lectures." For him, one cannot hope to understand "the system... without going to the roots—the real living and working people."

Despite these strongly held views, Mandel has never been accused of intolerance or imposing his views on students. Since his position is very much that of a minority in the field, he is virtually obliged to present the dominant views, something that is not true of establishment political scientists, who often pass off their views as "scientific" and the only ones worth discussing.

Since arriving in Montréal, Mandel has been involved in trade-union work, various socialist organizations, and peace and international solidarity activities, including, for a time, publication of a review in defence of democratic and trade-union rights in the Soviet bloc.

The fate of leftists in the McGill Political Science Department has not been encouraging. Two previous cases are especially noteworthy.

One case involved Sam Noumoff himself. Noumoff was the only other Marxist in the Department of Political Science during

Mandel's stay there, and subsequent to the decision not to offer Mandel the tenure-track post he was repeatedly cited by the university administration as proof that the department was pluralistic and did not discriminate against leftists.

But the truth was rather different. Noumoff had been in the department since 1967 but was granted tenure only in 1981, after an inordinate amount of time. On two occasions he was the object of attempts within the department to terminate his career at McGill. In 1974, the department decided to dismiss Noumoff for failing to complete his Ph.D. dissertation. By a vote of 7 v. 1, he was refused his request for a six-month extension, a flexibility shown in the case of other department members. Although the department ultimately reversed this decision, it was largely facilitated by the expressed opinion that, in any case, Noumoff would not complete his thesis. But not only did he defend his thesis within the allotted time, he received the Das Award from New York University's Political Science Department for the best dissertation on Asia.

In 1981, the department's Tenure and Promotion Committee voted 6 v. 5 with one abstention to deny Noumoff tenure. However, the *university's* Tenure Committee, the next level of decision, voted unanimously to overturn this decision and to grant tenure. The blatant discrepancy between these two decisions, based upon the same evidence, hardly requires comment.

In the second case, in 1969, the department offered a tenure-track post to Pauline Vaillancourt, who was completing her doctorate at Berkeley. When news of Vaillancourt's leftist politics began to reach McGill, the department attempted to renege on its offer, but finally decided against this, fearing legal complications and student protest. A student representative on the Appointments Committee reported that Professors Waller, Stein, and Nayar (all turn up later in the Mandel case) argued against the appointment because Vaillancourt was "bound to cause some kind of trouble." The impression he got from the meeting was one of a "political appointments committee."[1] In 1972, the department decided

---

[1] Marlene Dixon, *Things Which Are Done In Secret* (Montréal: Black Rose Books, 1976), p. 69.

not to renew Vaillancourt's contract. Vaillancourt brought charges against the department, alleging discrimination related to her political views and union activity at McGill. A CAUT inquiry concluded that her contract should be renewed. Besides serious procedural irregularities, it found glaring inconsistencies in the way Vaillancourt had been treated as compared to other junior faculty members in the same situation. In typical CAUT fashion, the "ungentlemanly" issue of discrimination was skirted by the committee, which claimed that it was unable to find a definition of the term.[2]

Mandel's political profile bears a striking resemblance to that of Noumoff and Vaillancourt, the main difference being their status at the university. Noumoff and Vaillancourt were both "insiders" with tenure-track contracts and therefore could make use of the established right to a review outside the department. Mandel, as an "outsider," was totally at the department's mercy. Moreover, this was a department that had learned through bitter experience how difficult it is to get rid of politically undesirable, but competent, colleagues once they had been granted an initial tenure-track appointment.

Noumoff's second point need not detain us for long. Mandel, who had studied in Israel, was fluent in Hebrew, and was married to an Israeli, was critical of Israeli policies, particularly regarding the Palestinians and the occupied territories. This position was at odds with that of several senior professors in the department, who were deeply involved in Israeli causes. Perhaps the problem can best be summarized in the words of Gretta Chambers, a journalist and a member of McGill's Board of Governors, quoted in *The McGill Daily* of September 12, 1980: "I think that had he been a good Jewish boy he would have been better liked." She was referring, she said, to a tendency of some members of the department to "like people with certain views on the Middle East."

Finally, on Noumoff's third point: in the winter of 1979-80, McGill had seen a strike of its maintenance employees, only the second strike in the university's history. Only a very small

---

[2] This case is documented in *Ibid.*

percentage of the faculty, mostly McGill Faculty Union (MFU)[3] members, respected the picket lines. In the Political Science Department, four out of some two dozen professors did not teach, despite threats by the administration to dock pay and take other measures. Mandel not only stayed out but was also highly visible on the picket lines, distributing leaflets that called for students and faculty to show their solidarity with the strikers.

Mandel's position on the strike stemmed from his conception of the university, which was directly at odds with the official ideology of "collegiality"—in his view, little more than a bad joke. Since the university administration ran the institution essentially like any business organization, the staff should be organized into a union which is kept at arm's length from the administration. This is why he supported the MFU's fight to win accreditation, in opposition to the "collegial" McGill Association, which includes among its members officers of the administration. Given the tendency of professors' unions to become conservative and corporatist, Mandel would have preferred to see a single union of all McGill employees which maintained close ties with representative student bodies. While this was not the MFU's position, its strong support for the maintenance workers' strike was in the same spirit.

Despite all this, Mandel's candidacy had overcome the opposition in the Appointments Committee, and there seemed good reason to believe it would do so in the department at large. After all, the Appointments Committee alone had access to all the confidential material in candidates' dossiers, and it was exceedingly rare for its recommendation to be rejected. As a Marxist and a political activist Mandel had had his share of troubles at Columbia, too; but in the end, so it seemed to him, it was the strength of his academic record that had proved decisive.

In addition, he had—or thought he had—Canadian immigration law and CAUT's "Canadianization" guidelines on his side. He was the only Canadian among the twenty-odd candidates seriously considered by the Appointments Committee, and both

---

[3] The following section of this chapter contains a brief history of staff organizations at McGill.

the law and CAUT called for the appointment of qualified Canadians.[4]

The departmental meeting began on the morning of April 29. That afternoon, Stephen Bornstein called Mandel to break the bad news: although the Appointments Committee had twice presented his name, his candidacy had been rejected by a vote of 13 v. 9 with one abstention. Instead, Professor Joan Debardeleben, an American, was chosen. Then Professor James Tully called to suggest that Mandel could "get them on the Canadian question," since the law requires the hiring of qualified Canadians where available. The issue had not even been discussed by the department. (Tully later testified that he had never encouraged Mandel to fight the decision nor did he support Mandel's complaint.) There were other calls from the student delegates, who expressed their shock and anger at the way in which the decision was taken: without any discussion of Mandel's qualifications and with no reasons offered for his rejection. Indeed, there appeared to have been a will to avoid any such discussion. The callers were unanimous in their view that the vote was politically biased and they urged Mandel to fight it.

Mandel waited to hear the department's reasons before deciding what course of action, if any, he should take. As a member of the Political Science Department, as the choice of the Appointments Committee, and as the sole Canadian, he felt he had a legitimate right to ask for these reasons.

The following day, Professor Frank Kunz, chair of the department, came to see Mandel in his office. His tone was apologetic. He emphasized the department's high regard for his qualifications, which had never been in doubt, and offered to do everything possible to make sure that he got a post elsewhere. The problem was, according to Kunz, that Mandel's research focus was too historical: the department needed someone with a more contemporary interest.

To Mandel, this sounded like a *post factum* rationalization. During his stay at McGill he had had no indication that anything

---

[4] The "Canadianization" issue is treated in the Conclusion. For the CAUT guidelines, see Appendix II.

either in his teaching approach or in his research made him a less desirable candidate. Nor was there anything in the advertisement to that effect. Moreover, he had been teaching contemporary politics and had informed Kunz well before the meeting that he was working on a research project with a contemporary theme. Mandel became even more suspicious when Kunz refused to give him a written version of his explanation, replying that he had "no record of the conversation." "The department followed its regular procedures in new appointments," and, as far as he was concerned, that closed the matter.

Meanwhile, new bits and pieces of information reached Mandel. A student reported that Professor Jerome Black had admitted that because of pressures in the department he had voted against Mandel although he considered him the superior candidate. Two students told Mandel of a conversation—at which they had been present—between Kunz and Gretta Chambers, in which Kunz spoke of the concern in the department over Mandel's personality and politics. Kunz also said that certain professors felt uncomfortable with Mandel. Chambers, whose daughter was a student in the department, herself told Mandel: "It's clear that you have been shafted." By now, a week after the decision, he was fully convinced of the injustice and determined to seek redress.

Although Kunz refused to offer Mandel any formal reasons for the rejection of his candidacy, he indicated that the dean of arts, Robert Vogel, wanted to speak with him. Having reached an impasse at the level of the department, Mandel decided to try the dean. But Vogel informed him that he had no right to an explanation. He himself could not explain the vote, which was carried out by secret ballot, but he assured Mandel that there was no bias against leftists in the department and cited the presence there of Professor Sam Noumoff. Vogel said he was "grubbing" for at least some part-time work for Mandel, though at some point he "would have to make a decision." But Mandel was already decided. He assured Vogel that he would see his grievance through to the end. No more was heard of Vogel's "grubbing."

Convinced that he had been offered a bribe and that there was no recourse within the university, Mandel made a last formal gesture in taking his complaint to the McGill Senate Staff Relations Committee. This committee refused to take the case because its mandate contained no specific reference to complaints relating to hiring.

This confirmed that there was no oversight or right of appeal in university hiring decisions. It was as if unfairness was conceivable in contract renewal and tenure decisions, which involved "insiders," after all, but was unthinkable in initial appointments. Or more likely: this refusal of appeal was an assertion by the university of the "right" of departments to freely use any criteria they saw fit in choosing their colleagues.

This claim had, in fact, been made by the McGill Political Science Department in 1974 to the CAUT committee of inquiry investigating Vaillancourt's complaint. Testifying before the committee, the chair of the department, Harold Waller, ingenuously asked whether it was not proper to use a probationary period (the first three-year contract) not to renew a member "who seems to create so many problems." The committee replied that "claims of non-collegiality [that would resurface again in the Mandel case] are entirely improper reasons for non-renewal."

By a curious twist of fate, the head of that inquiry was Dr. David Johnston, then dean of law at the University of Western Ontario. Johnston would also play a role in the Mandel case, but this time as principal of McGill and fierce opponent of any inquiry into the department his committee had censured only six years before.

The Academic Setting: Associations, Unions, Collegia

On June 6, 1951, the Canadian Association of University Teachers (CAUT) came into being. The proposal to set up the association arose "out of a widely felt need for a national association to represent the interests and viewpoints of the university teaching staffs in a world made up of highly organized groups."[5] Although

---

[5] Information on the founding of CAUT is taken from James Mallory, "Teachers' Union," *Queens Quarterly* 61:1 (Spring 1954).

CAUT was not intended as a federation of local staff associations, the founders recognized—and this has proven to be the case—that "much of the strength and vitality of the organization was certain to be located in local associations of teachers." In fact, the members of the McGill academic community who had entrepreneured the formation of the McGill Association of University Teachers (MAUT) in 1950 also helped promote the formation of CAUT.

There was no specific mention of setting standards for the hiring of new staff, but protecting academic freedom was clearly a dominant concern of CAUT's founders. In this spirit, when CAUT took up the Mandel case in 1980, they not only mandated the fact-finding committee to look into the situation surrounding the failure of McGill's Political Science Department to offer him an appointment, but they also wanted it "to recommend additions or amendments to CAUT guidelines to ensure fair hiring procedures in the universities." They seemed to be following in the grand tradition of the organization's "founding fathers."

Philosophically, CAUT reflected an ambivalent attitude towards organization along trade-union lines. In justifying the need for a national association, James Mallory of McGill's Political Science Department, whose idea of academic decorum led him to later withdraw his initial support for Mandel, observed that

> the university in North America, for all its strangely-named officials, its chancellors and vice-chancellors, regents, senates, and deans, is organized with the same emphasis on managerial flexibility and security of assets as Standard Oil or the Aluminum Company.... North American universities are bound to conform in their organization to the assumptions of the business world which bears and nourishes them. It is no use our saying that a university is a company of scholars who ought to run their own affairs. Such a conception is wholly foreign to our world.

However, in the same breath, in response to the criticism that a trade-union "frame of mind" and "trade-union tactics" are inappropriate for university teachers, Mallory allowed that "except perhaps for abnormal situations and very special objectives," the tactics of the strike would not be in the best interests of university professors, partly because a "university administration, if motivated by enlightened self-interest, will want what we want." In other words, despite comparisons with Standard Oil and the Aluminum Company, university professors, unlike typical union members, should not view their relationship with their employer as adversarial. In addition, although "the role of a university administration is to strike a balance between competing claims on the limited financial resources at their disposal," conflict need not result. "Very often (and it is remarkable how often this has happened in the brief history of Canadian staff associations) all that is necessary is to present a well-argued brief to persuade a finance committee to revise its scale of priorities." In the university, reasoned argument, the weapon of the intellectual, rather than the power of confrontation, will normally be used to settle disagreements. If, as Mallory observed, prior to the post-World War II expansion of universities "the harsh lines of power were appreciably softened in the small and close-knit academic community where mutual confidence and personal influence could usually obtain the benefits, though not the form, of academic independence," then in the large and more impersonal universities of the 1950s, enlightened administrators would turn to staff associations to help them govern.

It is more than thirty years since the formation of MAUT and CAUT. McGill is now the only Québec university without a certified bargaining unit. The majority of CAUT member associations also qualify as unions in the traditional sense of the term. Thus, in the 1980s, most Canadian university staff associations, recognizing the realities confronting post-World War II universities and building on the work of CAUT's founders, have accepted the need for the protection afforded by a collective agreement. In contrast, MAUT not only rejected the trade-union model but progressively gave up the independence from the university administration that was claimed at its formation in 1950.

In 1969, a group of McGill professors, dissatisfied with the representation provided by MAUT, formed a competing organization —the McGill Faculty Union (MFU), whose goal was to obtain accreditation under the terms of the Québec Labour

Code. In 1979, following a series of administration policy pronouncements designed to frustrate MFU organizing efforts, the MFU asked the Québec Labour Court to dissolve MAUT, charging that the McGill administration and the association colluded to thwart attempts by the MFU to establish contractural rights for McGill's academic staff. A two-year court case followed, with the final decision in 1981 favouring MAUT on the technical grounds that it was not an association of salaried employees as defined by the Labour Code. In his decision, Judge Claude Saint-Arnaud observed that the simultaneous presence of a "faculty association" and a union organization, pursuing fundamentally different objectives, creates a unique situation found in no other university. He also accepted the MFU argument that MAUT falsely gave the illusion of being a genuine negotiating agent, and that the university gave its support to this view. Almost thirty years to the day after the founding of CAUT, a Québec Labour Court judge declared that no genuine negotiations existed at McGill, and that MAUT was colluding with the university administration to prevent the unionization of its teaching staff.

McGill administrators and MAUT officers defend their relationship by portraying McGill's government as a collegium. In the words of McGill's principal and vice-chancellor, David Johnston,

> a definition of collegiality would not confine it to any specific political forum. Perhaps it is closest conceptually to a democratic system. As for any such participatory system, it is probably, above all, an attitude, an attitude which is shared by most members of the group and which rests in an unstable and precarious position as a result of its dependence on the collective perception of the group. It only works when most members of the group perceive that in fact the collective activities of the group conform most of the time to their idea of the common aims.[6]

---

[6] Taken from the speech delivered by Johnston at the ceremony installing him as McGill's Principal, February 8, 1980.

At the Human Rights hearing, the university's vice-principal for academic affairs, Samuel Freedman, stated:

> A university can be best described as a community of teacher scholars, engaged simultaneously in the pursuit of knowledge, and its dissemination to others, which governs itself in a collegial fashion. Collegiality is the attitude [that] the members of this community will participate in [the] decision-making process of the university and through their participation in its collective activities help to fashion common goals and attitudes. The collegial system is sufficiently flexible to permit the members of the university [community] to function as administrators while still carrying out their academic duties.

James Mallory's admonition, some thirty years earlier, that "it is no use our saying that a university is a company of scholars who ought to run their own affairs. Such a conception is wholly foreign to our world," has fallen on deaf ears. McGill's staff would rather accept the illusion proffered them by the administration and behave as if the "harsh lines of power" can be "softened" by the simple expedient of declaring the university government a collegium.

McGill's reality is an authoritarian power structure not subject to any internal, nor, as the Mandel case demonstrates, external control. Those who cooperate with the powers that be obtain personal benefits but cannot claim academic independence. Though Johnston feels that collegiality is "closest conceptually to a democratic system," a closer look at his definition reveals it to be nothing more than a false perception, a shared illusion of democratic rule in which there is no structural provision for real self-government. A Marxist would call it an ideology, and a corporatist one at that.

2 Obtaining a Hearing

In the weeks following the department's decision, Mandel consulted with both the McGill Association of University Teachers (MAUT) and the McGill Faculty Union (MFU). The response of MAUT's Grievance Committee chair, Professor Irving Gopnik, was polite if not particularly encouraging. He explained that the Canadian Association of University Teachers (CAUT) had no appeal procedure in initial hiring complaints and he advised against trying to appeal on the basis of CAUT guidelines giving preference to qualified Canadians.

It would not take long for MAUT's opposition to Mandel's appeal to emerge openly. Gopnik himself, an American by origin, like many members of McGill's staff, played a central role in drawing up the MAUT guidelines on hiring—which were eventually adopted by the McGill Senate—that rejected CAUT's position (see Chapter 6). (In all fairness, it should be noted that later, as a member of the Fédération des associations des professeurs des universités du Québecc (FAPUQ), MAUT paid the out-of-pocket expenses of the lawyer who FAPUQ briefly supplied to

47

Mandel, but only after it had tried unsuccessfully to stick Mandel, a member of MAUT during his stay at McGill, with the bill.)

Mandel's reception at the MFU was different. While it was made clear to him that the decision to pursue the complaint would have to be his own and should be made with circumspection, the MFU recognized the anomaly of a situation in which young academics had no recourse against discriminatory hiring practices and felt that Mandel's was about as strong a case as one could find with which to create a much needed precedent.

Other than the MFU and two professors from within the Political Science Department (Stephen Bornstein and Sam Noumoff), Mandel received no support from McGill staff members, though a number of academics wrote to the university from across Canada in support of an independent inquiry. The students, however, were a different matter. Both the Undergraduate and Graduate McGill Political Science Student Associations, as well as many individual students from other departments, demanded an inquiry into Mandel's allegations. *The McGill Daily*, in particular, was instrumental in keeping the issue alive in a university whose staff and administration tended to blame the victim for upsetting the collegial peace. As Dr. Nancy Partner of the History Department put it in a letter to *The Daily*:

> I have waited for this event to end, but not a month, not a week has passed without further public communication (by now fairly repetitious) on the subject.... In my experience, most academics cope with this kind of disappointment by treating themselves to a good wallow in self-pity, mixed with deeply libelous speculations on the moral and mental lives of the benighted selection committee that wronged them, all in the presence of a trusted friend—and then forget it.

Typically, it was not of the least concern whether Mandel's allegations were valid. The main thing was his lack of decorum in challenging the comforting illusion that the university functioned according to the lofty principles of academic freedom it officially professed. The Mandel case forced people to take sides and to risk something, however minimal. As few were willing to risk anything, the majority naturally saw Mandel as the source of their discomfort.

In a letter of June 18, Mandel formally requested an inquiry by the Academic Freedom and Tenure Committee (AF&T) of CAUT into McGill University's decision not to offer him the post in Soviet and East European politics. He cited the university's non-observance of the CAUT guidelines on "Canadianization":

> The appointment should be offered to the best-qualified Canadian who meets the stated requirements, unless the university-wide review committee, or if it does not exist, the senior academic body, is persuaded that the appointment in the case of a non-Canadian is justified.

Although Mandel had been the only Canadian considered and was judged the most qualified by the Appointments Committee, the university refused to justify or explain its decision.

But while the issue of "Canadianization" was clear, Mandel admitted that the absence of any formal statement of reason made the case in support of his second allegation, political bias, harder to prove. He proceeded to list the reasons that had been offered informally.

He reported a conversation that he had had with Professor Kunz, in which "he took great pains to emphasize the high quality of my teaching and research. The only reason he offered [for the failure to be appointed] was the historical orientation of my research." But, as noted before, that criterion was established after the fact, and Kunz was aware that Mandel had been teaching and researching contemporary politics, in addition to his work on the early Soviet period.

But Kunz had offered another reason to Gretta Chambers. Chambers had told Mandel that in Kunz's view he was not liked by certain members of the department who did not feel comfortable with him and that he thought that this had a great deal to do with the decision. Mandel also cited the letter of Anita Isaacs, a political science student and friend of Chambers' daughter who had been present at the conversation. According to Isaacs, Kunz also noted that there was concern over Mandel's "identity crisis: he wasn't sure whether he was a worker or a professor." Finally, Mandel cited the letter of another student, Jean Contratti, reporting that Professor Black had told her the meeting had been "orchestrated" and Mandel had not had "his day in court," and though he personally felt Mandel to be the most qualified candidate, he voted against his appointment because he "would have to live in the department for the next twenty years."[1]

Mandel concluded: "It is my firm conviction that if the Political Science Department were required to give reasons for its decision, I would be able to show that these reasons were not a valid basis for refusing me the position."

Dr. Sim, Executive Secretary of CAUT, replied for the AF&T, explaining that in light of the position

> Which CAUT has taken in similar appointment cases in the past... I cannot be particularly encouraging that CAUT will be able to assist you. Nevertheless, the facts of the case as you have outlined them to me... suggest that it would be useful for the committee to consider your request. It is in any event your right to bring a case to the attention of the committee if you wish to do so.

Sim's response typifies the CAUT approach in dealing with Mandel's complaint. At virtually every stage, its representatives let it be understood, without ever explaining, that there was not much it could do. But lest this appear to be a rejection of the organization's avowed *raison d'être*, they would graciously invite Mandel to invest more of his time and energy in seeking redress through the organization, always holding out at least the vague hope of action.

The AF&T committee discussed Mandel's request on July 18. The outcome of its deliberations was a letter from Sim to Principal David Johnston, asking for his "comments" on the appointment and, specifically, whether McGill had procedures

---

[1] Black was later to claim that these statements had been distorted.

to "ensure that qualified Canadians are carefully considered." But Sim hastened to assure Johnston, lest he misconstrue the request to mean that the AF&T committee's intervention was to be taken seriously, that the "Committee is not questioning the right of the Department of Political Science to make the recommendation it wishes." The allegation of political discrimination was not even mentioned.

Mandel himself did not receive any explanation from the AF&T committee for the course of action it had taken. In reply to his inquiries, Sim would only offer his own view which had to do with the strength of the evidence, and invite Mandel to resubmit his request to the committee at its next meeting in September. Mandel accepted the invitation, reminding Sim that the only relevant question pertaining to the "Canadianization" issue was whether or not, as the only Canadian candidate, he was qualified. This the department itself had admitted.

> As for the issue of bias, you did not really make clear to me how much and what kind of evidence would be sufficient to induce the committee to investigate. In fact, you stated that even the strongest evidence might not have induced the committee to act.

Replying to Sim's incredible suggestion that it would take a direct statement from a majority of the department admitting to discrimination to move the committee, Mandel described his futile attempts at collecting direct evidence. He cited the case of Professor Charles Taylor, Chambers' brother. Taylor had been a member of the committee that had interviewed Mandel in the summer of 1979 and recommended him for the visiting professor's post. He had called in sick the day of the appointment decision, but, according to his sister, had made inquiries among the other professors to learn why Mandel had been turned down. It was Chambers who sent Mandel to Taylor.

> I have asked Professor Taylor repeatedly. However, he refused to disclose the reasons to me on the grounds that I have no chance of winning.... He stated that to give me the reasons would only hurt the department... and he had to consider its welfare.

Taylor had been active that year at McGill, mobilizing support for Czechoslovak intellectuals, victims of political repression. Unfortunately for Mandel, he was neither Czechoslovak nor five thousand miles away.

Mandel concluded that only an inquiry by the AF&T committee could get at the real reasons. As far as he could tell, the committee's refusal to grant him this appeal was based solely on the fact that there was no precedent for it in an initial appointment. "The practical consequence is that departments are free in initial appointments to use criteria that have absolutely no place in an academic setting."

It was now September 1980. Mandel had been out of work for two months. His efforts to find employment in Montréal had thus far been unsuccessful. Montréal was his third city since graduation. He and his wife decided against uprooting the family once again. Mandel's ten-year-old daughter was settled in school, and his wife, a biologist, had finally found work.

At its meeting that month, the AF&T committee reversed itself and decided to propose an independent inquiry jointly sponsored by CAUT and McGill with a broad mandate to look into the circumstances surrounding the decision. Accordingly, on October 2, Drs. Sim and Foulks (chair of the AF&T committee), met with Principal Johnston. Johnston did not reply directly to the committee's proposal. Instead, he expressed concern for MAUT's position on this matter.

After their meeting with Johnston, Foulks and Sim spoke with Irving Gopnik, MAUT Grievance Committee chair. As a result of this meeting, they left Montréal confident of MAUT's support; as Sim wrote Johnston two weeks later, "we trust that you have now had an opportunity to discuss this matter with the McGill Association of University Teachers and are assured that there is general agreement that such an inquiry would be useful."

On October 9, however, the president of MAUT wrote Mandel, to the latter's consternation, that on the advice of the Grievance Committee, he had asked Principal Johnston "to undertake a formal verification of the procedures that were followed in considering your candidacy." By asking for an in-house inquiry limited to procedures, the MAUT executive (which included among its members the chair of the Department of Political Science) was serving notice of its intention to support the McGill administration in opposing an independent inquiry.

Thus, in his reply to Sim of October 22, Johnston first of all corrected him: "You indicate that there is general agreement that an inquiry with respect to a grievance of Dr. Mandel would be useful. I am not aware of such general agreement." Secondly, he ingenuously claimed not to know what Mandel's allegations were about, although Foulks and Sim had set these out at their October meeting with Johnston, just as Mandel had already done on several occasions to MAUT, the dean of arts, and the Senate Staff Relations Committee. Johnston expressed concern about

> the rights of faculty members in the Political Science Department who had participated in a rather democratic process to choose a colleague. They have had allegations directed against them in the media in a manner that raises some questions about observation of due process as a standard to protect them.

He concluded: "I regret that your letter does not reduce my uneasiness or help me to understand what, in essence, the complaint is about." Thus, for the first time in this case, the principle of "academic freedom" was invoked to block an inquiry into the alleged violation of that principle.

Sim repeated the allegations in a new letter to Johnston in which he once again proposed a jointly-sponsored, independent committee of inquiry whose decisons would be binding on both sides:

> We feel that an inquiry such as we have suggested is an effective way to protect the department. If Dr. Mandel's allegations are not justified, then the department and its members will be vindicated and the university will be seen to have responded in an effective way to the charges which have been made.

The work of the committee would be

carried on with discretion. The committee need not proceed in an adversarial fashion. It could, as have other CAUT committees of inquiry, conduct interviews with interested parties and give all those against whom negative information is provided, an opportunity to respond.... Persons with information to provide would not be "summoned" but would be given an opportunity to meet with the committee in private if they wished to do so.

Johnston chose not to respond to this. Rather, he took a completely new tack, noting that

> it is unusual for CAUT to request an investigation on behalf of one applicant amongst a great number for an initial tenure track appointment, on the basis that the applicant has alleged that individuals in the department were biased against him. Perhaps it is for this reason his request for an inquiry by the MAUT Grievance Committee and by the University Staff Relations Committee was refused.

In fact, Mandel had never requested an inquiry by MAUT, nor, for that matter, does MAUT conduct inquiries. Despite Mandel's protests, the university administration, with MAUT's tacit acquiescence, would continue to repeat this lie over the course of the next four years. The Staff Relations Committee's refusal, as noted earlier, had been based on the claimed absence of jurisdiction to inquire into initial appointments.

Once again, Johnston claimed not to have been informed by CAUT of the nature of Mandel's allegations: "We met with you on October 2nd. At that time you raised with us only the question of Dr. Mandel's application for an initial tenure track appointment and the MAUT policy on recruitment and appointment of Canadian citizens." The review of McGill's policy with respect to Canadian recruitment was now complete. He was enclosing a copy of a Senate resolution sponsored by MAUT obliging departments to advertise positions in Canadian publications while leaving them free to advertise abroad as well. This resolution, which, in fact, did not even mention the desirability of hiring qualified Canadians, and made no provision for a body to review foreign appointments, was a direct rejection of CAUT guidelines.

Johnston did acknowledge in passing having received Mandel's allegations, though he claimed these were only in "partial form." In what proved to be a favourite tactic, he gingerly passed on to a new complaint.

> There has been a widespread publicity campaign generated presumably by Dr. Mandel, perhaps with your knowledge. That campaign which made damaging allegations made it difficult to inquire dispassionately and thoughtfully into the matter.

Again, Johnston was being somewhat less than truthful. In his previous letter, cited above, he had vigorously denied that there was, or had ever been, a will at McGill "to inquire dispassionately and thoughtfully in the matter."

In any case, he continued,

> it is now impossible for me to consider acting as you suggest on these allegations. Two days ago I learned from the department chair that an agency of the provincial government has decided to investigate Dr. Mandel's complaint.... Thus there is now an external investigation in place. Since the matter is *sub judice* I cannot comment further. I find it unfortunate that you would ask me to consider an inquiry... while at the same time the complainant, presumably with your knowledge, was calling for an external investigation by a government body.... The Human Rights inquiry is not the procedure the university would have preferred if any inquiry were warranted. Nevertheless, it is the type of inquiry that has been requested and obtained. We must all, now, simply abide the outcome.

In reality, the Human Rights Commission inquiry was still ten months off, and McGill was preparing to challenge the commission's decision to investigate. Mandel had requested this inquiry only after the AF&T committee's initial refusal in July to itself inquire into his allegations. As for the alleged impropriety of two parallel inquiries, the Human Rights Commission itself later assured CAUT that there was no conflict between them.

Sim replied in detail to Johnston's complaints and accusations. Responding to the principal's claim that the allegations were in "partial form," he wrote: "The statement is, I think, as complete and thorough as it is possible or necessary at this stage." As for the publicity campaign on Dr. Mandel's behalf, CAUT's knowledge of it "is no greater than your own." Sim especially took issue with Johnston's claim—which was being repeated in McGill's letters to academics who had written in support of an independent inquiry—that when he met with Sim and Foulks in early October they discussed only the "Canadianization" issue: "Your letter to me of October 22 (page 1, paragraph 4) makes it clear, however, that we discussed as well issues of bias and discrimination." Finally, Sim answered Johnston's remarks about the external inquiry:

> Though we knew that Dr. Mandel, as was his right, had asked the Québec Human Rights Commission for assistance, I learned only on November 14 that the QHRC would conduct an investigation. The CAUT proposal to you was made earlier in good faith when it was not known whether the commission would take up the case. I note your view that a commission investigation is not what the University would have preferred. The QHRC investigation could presumably be stayed if agreement could be reached on a joint CAUT-McGill committee of inquiry. This was done, I believe, in the Vaillancourt case some years ago.[2]

Two days later, Sim wrote to McGill Vice-Principal Academic Eigel Pedersen:

> It is a source of great disappointment to the CAUT Academic Freedom and Tenure Committee that the issues in the Mandel grievance have been obscured by excessively legalistic debating points. The Committee hoped for and would still respond promptly to any proposal the University wishes to make for co-operatively resolving this unfortunate dispute.

---

[2] When the Political Science Department refused to renew Pauline Vaillancourt's contract, she took her complaint to the Québec Labour Relations Board as well as to CAUT. McGill agreed to a binding joint CAUT-McGill inquiry on the condition that the appeal to the Labour Relations Board be dropped. Vaillancourt accepted this condition.

Johnston replied on December 19 to the offer to stay the Human Rights inquiry:

> Our university solicitors advise me that the Québec Human Rights Commission is seized of Dr. Mandel's complaint, that the investigation is now in course, that the case is *sub judice*, and that I should not comment further. Much as I regret this investigation, it will serve as the external inquiry for which your Association and Dr. Mandel have been seeking [*sic*]. I will therefore assume that the matter is closed between us and we will await the outcome of the Human Rights Commission deliberations.

It was already February 1981. After six months without work, Mandel was now teaching part-time as a *chargé de cours* in political science at the Université du Québec à Montréal (UQAM). *Chargés de cours*s at UQAM, who teach half of the university's courses, sign a contract for each course, for which they are paid about one third the salary of regular staff.

Despite Mandel's urgings that the AF&T committee proceed unilaterally with an inquiry, the committee renewed its proposal to Johnston, again offering to stay the Human Rights inquiry. Johnston replied: "Our university's solicitor has already spent a very considerable amount of time in communication and correspondence with the Human Rights Commission on this unfortunate complaint." He again raised the bogey of academic freedom, expressing concern that the commission would be questioning professors about how they voted at the departmental assembly: "This university does not welcome a procedure which trespasses on professors' privacy in this way but it is my understanding that you contemplated a similar procedure for the joint CAUT-McGill committee of inquiry you proposed."

In fact, as Sim had already written in a letter of November 6 and would reiterate on February 23,

> those who wished to meet with the committee would be given an opportunity to do so. They would not (and should not) be compelled to do so.... It is difficult to see how the CAUT suggestion that serious charges be examined carefully

can be construed as implying lack of sensitivity for the rights of the members of the Department of Political Science.

Johnston continued:

> You must appreciate that Dr. Mandel has made extremely serious and damaging charges against colleagues in the University which they conclude have no basis in fact.... I want you to understand that we have been troubled by these attacks directed towards professors in this University and we are somewhat puzzled that your Committee does not demonstrate a similar sensitivity and concern for their rights.

He concluded: "We view the Human Rights Commission inquiry as the appropriate external inquiry, one which would fully and exhaustively satisfy the concerns of your Committee and Dr. Mandel."

Only three days later, McGill lawyers sent off a brief to the Human Rights Commission, claiming that "the complaint cannot be regarded as having enough prima facie evidence to warrant an investigation and should be dismissed at this stage." So much for the "appropriate external inquiry."

Mandel continued to urge the AF&T committee to proceed unilaterally, arguing that to refuse to investigate a complaint that the committee had admitted deserved a hearing, only because McGill would not cooperate, was to

> make the defence of academic freedom dependent upon the good will of university administrations. The implication of Principal Johnston's position is that remedy through the CAUT against the university administration can be vetoed by the administration itself. That would mean, obviously, that there is practically never a remedy available.

The committee backed down, however. In March 1981, it renounced the idea of a CAUT-sponsored inquiry, offering to request *amicus curiae* status at the Human Rights inquiry. In conversation with the committee's new chair, Dr. Jill Vickers, Mandel made it clear that he considered this an empty gesture, all the more so since the Human Rights inquiry was being challenged by McGill and might never take place. It was at this point that Vickers hinted at her dissent from the committee's majority position and indicated to Mandel that he had a right to go over the committee's head directly to the CAUT board that was meeting in a few days.

Mandel made his request to the board. When he appeared before it in Ottawa on March 15, 1981, the decision had already been taken to establish an inquiry without McGill's cooperation that would answer directly to the board, and not, as was general practice, to the committee. It seemed almost too good to be true. But for the moment the only indication that the board had not acted purely out of principle was the slightly foul odour that drifted in from behind the scenes, where, in a *quid pro quo*, Vickers was forced to resign her position as chair of the AF&T committee.

It had taken nine months, but Mandel had established his right to an appeal. A few weeks later, the Québec Human Rights Commission rejected McGill's challenge, reaffirming that there were indeed sufficient grounds to proceed with an inquiry. By playing both sides against the middle, McGill ended up with not one, but two unwanted inquiries. Despite the excruciating slowness of the process, Mandel's months of effort seemed to have paid off.

3 The Hearings

More than a year had passed since Mandel had brought his complaint to CAUT. He had to look forward to another term of teaching as cheap labour at UQAM. He was also working ten hours a week as research associate with the Labour Studies Group at McGill's Centre for Developing-Area Studies (CDAS). This group had a team grant from the Social Science and Humanities Research Council (SSHRC) which allowed it to hire Mandel without McGill's approval, but this did not prevent the CDAS Directorate (political scientist Tom Bruneau was director at the time, and Tom Eisemon of the Faculty of Education was his assistant) from harassing Mandel by collecting his books and papers and locking them in the dean's safe.

Mandel's main hope for the coming year was a grant proposal to SSHRC that would allow him to continue his research on the Soviet working class. In April 1982 he was to learn that he had been awarded a three-year grant which would give him four months salary each year as well as travelling expenses. Meanwhile, there was the CAUT hearing to consider.

Setting the Stage

CAUT, as is normally the case, was very conscious of the need to protect the rights of all concerned when investigating a charge of discrimination, not only for reasons of equity but as recognition that CAUT lacked legal power and needed the university's cooperation to resolve any conflict. In addition, both Victor Sim and Dale Gibson, who was chair of the fact-finding committee, were aware that CAUT was breaking new ground in investigating a complaint relating to an initial appointment. This required even more caution about procedures than might normally have been the case. Finally, Principal Johnston's behaviour up to that point made it painfully obvious that McGill would grasp at any chance to undermine the credibility and legitimacy of the inquiry into Mandel's charges.

On August 20, 1981, CAUT sent out a notice announcing the establishment of a "Fact-Finding Committee on Discrimination or Unfair Hiring Practices in Making University Appointments." Dale Gibson, from the University of Manitoba, was to chair the committee, which included André Côté of Laval University and Keith Johnstone of the University of Saskatchewan. The committee's Terms of Reference were the following:

1. ...to indicate the standard of fairness which should be observed in assessing applications for appointments in Canadian universities with a view to ensuring non-discrimination and fair hiring practices.

2. ...to suggest criteria which might be used by CAUT in determining when it is appropriate to intervene in cases where allegations of discrimination in appointment decisions have been made.

3. ...to recommend additions or amendments to CAUT guidelines to ensure fair hiring procedures in the universities, and

4. ...to examine the circumstances surrounding the decision of the Department of Political Science at McGill University not to offer a new appointment to Dr. David Mandel and to advise the CAUT Board whether the procedures used and the decision resulting from those procedures were inadequate in any way and, if so, to

indicate whether the procedures resulted in unfairness to Dr. Mandel and, if necessary, to suggest an appropriate remedy.

The committee was to conduct interviews on the McGill campus October 2 and 3, 1981.

The investigative procedures to be followed were fairly standard. As set out in the CAUT guidelines they specified that the committee would initially proceed by means of personal interviews with individuals having pertinent information or viewpoints. Mandel would be made aware of the content, but not the source, of adverse information received. He would also have the opportunity to rebut such information.

Although the committee of inquiry might move on to hear formal testimony before observers, it would not afford the opportunity for cross-examination to any person appearing before the committee or to observers.

The expectation was that the committee would determine whether the university's decision was reached fairly and was rationally supported on both procedural and substantive grounds in the light of CAUT principles.

Sim anticipated a problem from the outset. In a letter to Gibson,[1] he noted:

> Dr. Mandel's complaint is also being investigated by the Québec Human Rights Committee. It is at least partly for this reason that the McGill administration declined to consider alternative means proposed by CAUT to consider grievance and its implications. It is possible that the University administration will decline to co-operate with your committee for the same reason. The CAUT Board feels, however, that the issues raised by the Mandel case are sufficiently important to establish the fact-finding committee and to authorize you to proceed even if full co-operation from all those concerned at McGill is not forthcoming.

---

[1] At the time, Professor Gibson was chair of the Manitoba Human Rights Commission.

> ...We expect that the McGill Association of University Teachers will assist the work of your committee by making local arrangements and by scheduling appointments with persons you wish to meet. The President of the MAUT is Professor John Harrod (Physics).... You should get in touch with Professor Harrod to co-ordinate your visits to the campus....
>
> Under the usual CAUT procedures, a copy of your draft report will be sent to the interested parties for comment. When a draft report has been completed, please send it to me and I will send it to the interested parties for comment. I will provide all the comments to you so that you may prepare a final report which will also be sent to the interested parties.

Hoping to obtain university cooperation, Gibson contacted Johnston and set out his view of the hearing. He rejected Johnston's contention that Mandel's complaint was *sub judice* before the Québec Human Rights Commission:

> Our task is entirely different than that of the Human Rights Commission. One of our functions, for example, will be to enquire into the validity of Dr. Mandel's complaint that his non-appointment involved a non-compliance with the CAUT guidelines on "Canadianization and the University." That complaint is not before the Human Rights Commission.

On the issue of political discrimination, too, he argued:

> The Commission's role differs markedly from ours. It must decide whether there has been a breach of the law—the *Québec Charter of Human Rights and Freedoms*, and, if so, what remedies, if any, to recommend.... We have not been asked to deal with that legal question, but rather with the much broader question of whether "the procedures used and the decision resulting from those procedures were inadequate in any way." To the extent that we will be considering allegations of political discrimination, our criteria will be those which are consonant with the notion of academic freedom as generally understood in the Canadian academic community, rather than those of any statute.

Finally, he pointed to the tasks assigned to the committee in its terms of reference:

> These have to do with general recommendations concerning fair hiring practices, CAUT involvement in such matters, and the possibility of amending or adding to existing CAUT guidelines to cover such matters. Although these general recommendations will not involve the Mandel case directly, the facts of that case may provide, by way of illustration, insights that will assist us in formulating satisfactory proposals.

In conclusion, he asked for the cooperation of Johnston and his staff, assuring him that there was no legal obstacle to their proceeding, that they would "do nothing to interfere with or prejudice the Commission's investigation or any judicial proceedings that might subsequently be commenced." He informed Johnston that his committee had requested the Human Rights Commission to inform them if in its view there would be any legal impediment to their proceeding.

The care taken by the committee is reflected in Gibson's note to Joan Debardeleben, the person hired by the Political Science Department.

> Although our task does not involve you directly, we feel that you, as the person who received the appointment Dr. Mandel was denied, ought to be fully informed of our activities. We also want to assure you, before we have even begun our investigation, that if we were to decide that Dr. Mandel's allegations are well founded and that he is accordingly entitled to some remedy, we would include in our report a recommendation that no such remedy should prejudice the rights you now have as a member of the McGill University Faculty.
>
> ...There is one piece of information that we would be very grateful to receive from you. We have a copy of Dr. Mandel's curriculum vitae, but we do not have those of the other candidates. If it would not be inconvenient, we would greatly appreciate your making available to us a copy of your curriculum vitae.

Finally, Gibson wrote to potential interviewees.

CAUT proposed to McGill University that the two organizations conduct a joint investigation of these allegations. When the University declined to take part in joint investigation, the CAUT Board decided to establish a committee of its own for the purpose.

...We should stress that so far as the Mandel case is concerned, our visit to McGill is for fact-finding purposes only. We are not soliciting group presentations, briefs, arguments, or expressions of support for one side or the other. We are interested only in facts relating to the circumstances surrounding the decision not to appoint Dr. Mandel.

We have been led to believe that you might have information that would assist us in our task. We are accordingly writing to request your assistance. Would you agree to meet with us during our visit to McGill and discuss any such information that you may have? We would be very grateful if you would.

The University Resists

It was not long before the university made its position known in a letter to Professor Gibson from McGill's dean of arts, Michael Maxwell. Better than any other statement from the university, it illustrates the hypocritical use of "academic freedom" as a shield against impartial inquiry into an alleged violation of that same principle. We therefore quote it, as well as Gibson's response, at length.

Maxwell began by accusing the fact-finding committee of intending to do more than find and report the facts.

> You have, in effect, been asked to declare whether Dr. Mandel should have been hired instead of the successful candidate. You and your committee are therefore acting as though you were empowered under the charter and statutes of McGill to make recommendations on appointments. I cite as further evidence that this is your intent a letter dated 20 August 1981 written by you to Dr. Debardeleben in which you state that you have Dr. Mandel's *curriculum vitae* but you lack those of the other candidates and that you would like to have Dr. Debardeleben's. This indicates to me that you

have the desire to compare two or more sets of *curriculum vitae* and make a judgement between them. This, in my opinion, involves far more than investigating the fairness of the procedures and involves making an academic judgement about who ought to have been appointed to the advertised position at McGill. Furthermore, not one of those who would be making this judgement has an appointment in a department of political science. I stress here that what counts is your apparent intent. It is going to be difficult for you to procure all the *c.v.*s involved, but your failure to obtain them does not alter your stated desire to see at least two of them.

Further support for the conviction that the true aims of your committee are to make a recommendation for an appointment at McGill, including an academic assessment of the various candidates, is the statement in the guidelines that are intended to govern your committee. I refer to paragraph "f" in those guidelines which states that you are expected to determine whether "the university's decision was fairly reached and was rationally supported on both procedural and *substantive grounds*..." (my emphasis). Substantive grounds can only mean that your committee, made up of a lawyer, a philosopher and a specialist in English literature, is about to weigh the relative merits of one political scientist against one or more others; we have no means of knowing how many as we are not told.

Dean Maxwell reveals his sense of the administration's prerogatives:

> I note, moreover, that you do not even mention... that you had already written to a member of the faculty asking for her *c.v.* I must vigorously protest this action which shows, in my opinion, a contempt for the duly appointed officers of this university; it seems to me that the Dean had the right to know if the qualifications of a member of his faculty are to be, or are likely to be, examined for other purposes than employment. You, without any status in this university, have begun to interfere in the affairs of this faculty.

The very legitimacy of the CAUT board's intervention is then questioned:

> By what warrant do you act? It appears that you and two others claim to have a right to establish the "standards of fairness" which should apply in certain circumstances throughout Canada. This, to say the least, is a large claim and, as a citizen of this country, I would like to know why I or anyone else should accept your "standards of fairness"? Here, there seems to me, to be an issue not only of academic freedom, but of fundamental liberty within a free society.
>
> ...It has been the right of a citizen since the eighteenth century to read the proceedings of the assembly that sets up a judicial body that affects his rights. On the surface, at least, it looks as though the one body within CAUT that is charged with protecting academic freedom and tenure [the Academic Freedom and Tenure Committee] has not recently expressed an opinion on the issues your committee is to examine. If this is so, it is odd. Am I right? If I am, please tell me on what other specific occasions the board alone has ordered the institution of such a committee.

Maxwell then moved on to what he called substantive issues.

> First, you refer to an alleged failure to follow guidelines on Canadianization.... I am informed that the immigration authorities of both Québec and Canada approved our procedures. The matter, therefore, has already been judged in our favour unless you are attempting to impose additional criteria in which case, I again question your right to do so.
>
> Second, you raise the charge of political discrimination. This is a charge that is presently being investigated by the Québec Commission on Human Rights, and a hearing is in the process of being scheduled.... It is surely possible that a decision your committee reaches could influence the decision of the Commission or *vice versa* and this might prejudice either Dr. Mandel's or the university's case. Let me add that the university is obliged and ready to receive the Commission's ruling on the matter, it being a duly constituted body under the law.
>
> Finally, I come to the question of your own procedures.... First, the procedures you outline cannot, in my view, produce

all the evidence that is necessary to lead to an informed opinion. The evidence you collect will depend on chance and whim and any report based on it would be deemed highly suspect, whatever its result, by any reputable scholar. Second, a paper entitled "The Observance of Natural Justice by University Tribunals" (1980) signed by five lawyers in Montréal (Yarofsky, Fish, Zigman, Issacs and Daviault) contains the following passage (p. 25):

> It is contrary to the rules of natural justice for a tribunal to consider information obtained from or representation made by one party to a proceeding in the absence of the other without, at the very least, revealing such information or representations to the latter and affording him or her the opportunity to correct or meet any adverse statement made.

How do you propose to meet this requirement of natural justice?

Finally, if the procedures you outline were used at McGill in the determination of tenure or appointment cases, there would quickly be a cry of "unfair"; indeed, there well might be an appeal to CAUT. If, with these procedures, you are attempting to guard academic freedom, who is to protect us from our guardians?

...I have to ask for a careful answer to all the questions I have raised. In the absence of satisfactory answers, I can only say that I do not accept your right to investigate the matters you list, and I protest against both your interference in the affairs of the faculty, the apparent attempt to deprive the university of the right to make its own appointments, and the procedures you have adopted in pursuing your objectives. I am deeply concerned that this type of process is leading to a situation in which universities and those who work in them are subjected to a variety of persecution.

...I urge you, in the light of the issues I have raised, to abandon your plans for a visit to McGill until my questions are answered. If you persist in coming, no doubt some people will appear before you. If these should include university officers, they may well be appearing under protest at the whole nature of your inquiry as well as your procedures. Others may also indicate that you and your colleagues represent a greater threat to their academic freedom than any action by the administration of this university. My last question is, if this is the case, where do they seek redress?

It would be hard to find a more blatantly self-serving use of "academic freedom" to prevent action against its alleged violation. Maxwell's hypocrisy is obvious when one recalls that the university opposed *any* inquiry, whatever its terms and procedures. But this did not stop Maxwell from claiming that the university had accepted the Human Rights inquiry. Yet the procedures adopted by CAUT were considerably more cautious than the Human Rights Commission's in relation to the claimed rights of the Political Science Department staff. Moreover, McGill was to use the same tactic against the Human Rights investigation (once it went ahead over its objections), with the Senate accusing the inquiry of blatant violations of academic freedom in inquiring into the political views of staff. (See Chapter 6.)

Professor Gibson's response refuted Dean Maxwell's accusations while trying to allay his fears. Gibson stressed that the committee was not an adjudicative tribunal.

> I understand that the CAUT requested McGill University to collaborate with it in creating such a tribunal to deal with Dr. Mandel's complaints, but that the University declined to do so. Faced with disturbing allegations by one of its members and the unwillingness of the University involved to join in a jointly sponsored adjudication of the complaints, CAUT decided to establish an Inquiry Committee of its own to investigate the allegations as best it can on behalf of CAUT, and to report its findings to CAUT....
>
> ...We are simply an advisory committee to the body that appointed us. We have no power to compel anyone to meet with us and no mandate to determine anyone's rights. If we are able, after our investigations and deliberations, to arrive at conclusions on any or all of the questions we have been asked to consider, our conclusions will carry only the weight of their own persuasiveness. If there are some at McGill who do not wish to meet with our Committee they are as free to decline our invitation as others are to accept. If there are some who find our conclusions erroneous or unacceptable, they will be as free to disregard them as those

who are persuaded by them will be to seek their implementation through appropriate channels.

Gibson also rejected the dean's accusation that CAUT or the members of the committee had prejudged the issues they had been asked to consider:

> Speaking for myself, I simply don't have enough information about any of the questions we have been asked, to form any opinion about them even if I wanted to. My colleagues on the Committee are in the same situation, and no one at CAUT has said or done anything to my knowledge that would indicate prejudgement. You ask at one point how you can trust the objectivity of our Committee. We have no certificates of trustworthiness to offer, other than our personal and professional reputations. In the long run, the only really effective way to assess our objectivity will be to examine our report.

The rest of Gibson's letter addresses specific points raised by Maxwell:

> It is not our task to advise CAUT or anyone else as to who should have been appointed. Our task in relation to the Mandel case ends when we have reported our findings on the "political bias" and "Canadianization" questions. It is true, as you point out... that one of our guidelines asks us to express an opinion as to whether "the University's decision was fairly reached and was rationally supported on both procedural and substantive grounds...." It does not follow from that mandate, however, that we have been asked to state who should have been appointed.
>
> ...What I find difficult to understand in your letter is the statement that requesting a professor's c.v. from the professor directly "shows... a contempt for the duly appointed officers of this University." I would have regarded it as questionable to ask anyone other than the professor concerned for a curriculum vitae. In my view, a curriculum vitae is the personal record of an academic, access to which ought to be controlled by the professor, not by "duly appointed officers" of the professor's current university.

...You accuse us of claiming "to have a right to establish the 'standards of fairness' which should apply in certain circumstances throughout Canada".... We claim only the right to express an opinion on the questions we have been asked. You point out... that the issue is one of "fundamental liberty within a free society," and I'm sure you would therefore agree that the members of our Committee have the liberty to express opinions about matters of concern to the Canadian university community and to society in general.

...You ask a number of questions about the background to the establishment of our Committee. I don't know the answer to most of your questions. I know only that, as I stated in my earlier letter, our Committee was appointed by the CAUT Board. I don't frankly understand the significance of your other questions, but if you regard them as important, I would suggest that you refer them to Dr. Sim or Dr. Savage at CAUT.

...I don't agree with you that mere compliance with provincial and federal immigration laws disposes of the question. Surely Canada's major association of university teachers has the "fundamental liberty within a free society" to express the view that universities should observe more than the minimal requirements of the law in this or in any other regard, and to ask a committee advising it to report on whether the practices in a given university appear to comply with the standards it regards as advisable.

...In our view, our inquiry does not duplicate the investigation being conducted by the Human Rights Commission, and would not interfere with it in any way. The standards laid down by the provincial Human Rights legislation are very different, at least in their phraseology, than the standards of fair appointment we have been asked to consider. In order to ensure that we do not interfere in any way with the Human Rights Commission proceeding, we have taken the precaution of informing the Commission of our plans and requesting its view as to whether we are likely to interfere with its work....

I don't share the view that you express... that the CAUT guidelines under which we will be operating "cannot... produce all the evidence that is necessary to lead to an informed opinion." It is possible, of course, that we will not be able to obtain enough information to arrive at an informed opinion. We are not prepared, at this stage, however, to dismiss the possibility that we will be able to do the job properly under the guidelines we have been asked to follow. You refer to the need to observe natural justice in proceedings by "university tribunals".... I agree entirely that it would be wrong to ignore the dictates of natural justice in the inquiries we are making on behalf of CAUT. The statement you quote indicates the desirability of letting everyone affected know the nature of the allegations made concerning them, and giving them an opportunity to reply. You ask how we intend to meet this requirement of natural justice. I refer you to the guidelines, where you will find... instructions designed to do precisely that. If there are other improvements in our procedures that you would deem advisable, I would be delighted to learn of them and to discuss with my colleagues the possibility of adopting them.

Gibson concluded by gently calling into question the authenticity of McGill's commitment to academic values.

I was deeply disturbed at the thought that other members of the Canadian university community would regard it as "interference," "persecution," and a "threat to... academic freedom" for three Canadian scholars to visit McGill University and inquire on behalf of Canada's major national university teachers organization, about serious allegations of political bias at McGill. I have always thought that the spirit of free and honest inquiry that we are all expected to display in our scholarship should also be welcome in our approach to other aspects of university life. Your letter could be read as implying a different view. If it does, there is little chance that we will be able to reach any consensus other than an agreement to disagree.

McGill, however, was not to be mollified. Maxwell carried McGill's adversarial approach to the inquiry a step further in a letter to potential witnesses, offering the services of the university's solicitor, Jules Duchesneau, who, "along with a court stenographer, is willing to accompany any staff member who wishes to have a legal representative."

Many members of the Political Science Department took Maxwell up on his offer. In fact, as would become clear in later testimony before the Québec Human Rights Commission, members of the department met as a group with McGill's lawyer prior to October 2 and 3 in order to discuss their appearance before the committee and to get their stories straight.

McGill, like all Québec universities, was going through a budget squeeze at this time. Yet money was no object when it came to defending itself against an inquiry into alleged wrongdoing by its own staff. Duchesneau, a Queen's Council, was present for every moment of the Human Rights Commission hearing and spent numerous hours at the non-judicial inquiry conducted by CAUT. But Mandel, except for limited legal time made available by FAPUQ (the provincial professors' association), was without professional legal council. This imbalance underlines the problems confronting an individual who must defend his or her rights against an establishment institution supported by public funds and a huge private endowment.

The report of the fact-finding committee commented on Maxwell's offer of the services of the university's solicitor.

> Apparently unimpressed by our repeated disavowals of adjudicative authority, Dean Maxwell seems to have been determined to clothe us with a judicial aura.

In general, the committee described its reception at McGill as "civil but frosty."

> Principal Johnston agreed to meet us, but only "under protest" and "as a matter of courtesy." The letter in which he informed us of that fact also indicated a belief that we had already determined the existence of *"prima facie* evidence of infringement of the academic freedom of Dr. Mandel...."
>
> Dr. Johnston's letter also expressed "sympathy" with the objections raised to our visit in a remarkable letter sent to the chairman of our committee by Dean M.D. Maxwell. Space precludes full discussion of Dean Maxwell's astonishing accusations.

MAUT, even though it was a member of CAUT, was not to be outdone. It displayed its usual zealous solidarity with the McGill administration. In a letter to potential witnesses, MAUT itself now reiterated McGill's lie that it had conducted an inquiry, and linked a call for cooperation with the CAUT fact-finding committee with a not-so-veiled attack on it.

> Since the MAUT has not found evidence to suggest impropriety in the procedures surrounding the decision of the Political Science Department not to offer a new appointment to Dr. David Mandel, it has maintained a neutral position on the matter. From this position we have seen fit to give Dr. Mandel whatever help he has asked to pursue his grievance and we have cooperated with the various bodies involved in the pursuance of this case.
>
> The other face of our neutrality is a concern for the *rights* of those members of the Political Science, and other departments, who have been drawn into the case and have been asked to appear before the CAUT Fact-Finding Committee. The MAUT is anxious that *staff members* be fully aware of their *rights* and *obligations* with regard to testimony before the Fact-Finding Committee. We fully endorse the notion that full cooperation with such a committee of enquiry is necessary if justice is to be seen to be done. We also recognize that committees of this kind may exert, or seem to exert, their own kind of *tyranny*. The MAUT is happy to give whatever *help* it can to make the interaction between its members and the committee of enquiry a constructive experience.

In its report the fact-finding committee sadly observed that this letter, written by MAUT President J.F. Harrod, "did much to undo our preliminary efforts to relieve anxiety based on misconceptions of our functions." And it concluded:

> We think it important to record our disappointment with the attitude displayed by McGill University, its officers and many of its academic staff toward a sincere attempt by three independent academics on behalf of Canada's largest organization of university teachers to make inquiries about very serious allegations of interference with academic freedom. It must not be forgotten that our inquiry was not launched until after the University, in spite of urging by CAUT, had refused to make Dr. Mandel's charges the subject of an impartial academic inquiry. McGill University is one of

Canada's oldest and most celebrated institutions of higher learning. We have no doubt that its faculty and officers unanimously espouse the principle that scholarly work should involve the open and fearless pursuit of truth. To find them denying the appropriateness of that principle when applied to an inquiry into the propriety of their own administrative actions is deeply disturbing. Apart from all other considerations involved, one would think that individuals of the competence of the administrators and scholars involved would be wise enough to realize that such an attitude may convey the impression to outsiders that McGill has something to hide.

Testimony

The CAUT fact-finding committee heard testimony in the absence of Professor Mandel; witnesses' appearance before it was entirely voluntary, no opportunity was provided for cross-examination, and the committee specifically refrained from posing questions as to how department members voted or their motivation. The Québec Human Rights Commission hearing, however, operated under none of these constraints. Its verbatim transcripts of testimony provide a clear indication of McGill's strategy against allegations of wrongdoing. We therefore now turn to this testimony.

We Can't Tell You—It Would Destroy Western Civilization

The university hoped to limit the scope of the inquiry by claiming that witnesses could not be asked how they voted on the appointment. If witnesses did not have to indicate how they voted, then they could not be asked to explain the reasoning behind their vote. This strategy was revealed by Professor Frank Kunz, chair of the Political Science Department and the first hostile witness to appear before the commission.

C. Trudel [chair of the hearing]: Did you approve his candidature [*sic*] or were you against?

> Kunz: ...I am not sure whether I should reveal how I personally voted at that time, or subsequent times, about appointments.... Academic appointments are predicated upon elements of confidentiality, and that includes, in our case, secrecy of ballot.

Trudel rejected this contention, clearly seeing the logic of Kunz's position:

> Mandel... alleges an infringement of his basic rights, and one must discover what really happened.... If we respected this rule of confidentiality... we would not be able to learn the... motivations of each participant in the decision-making process.... I think these people... must assume their responsibilities in relation to the choices they have made, to give the explanations that are called for.

McGill was not ready to voluntarily assume its responsibilities. Their lawyer indicated that the university was prepared to take the matter to Superior Court. This could have taken years and time was obviously on McGill's side. To save time, the commissioner offered to delay a final decision to let McGill present more elaborate and detailed arguments. It was in this context that Vice-Principal Academic Samuel Freedman appeared before the Commission.

After reading into the record McGill's definition of collegiality and academic freedom,[2] which, he claimed, were closely interconnected and universally held in Western civilization (though, when asked on different occasions, he was unable to cite a single source to support his claim), Freedman concluded:

> The notion of confidentiality in making selection is important for the protection of the candidates as well as for the University and for the notion of academic freedom. If an individual feels obligated to a particular group of people who he knows voted for him, or he feels hostile to a particular group of people who he knows voted against him in open vote, then this interferes with the concept of academic freedom.

---

[2] See Chapter 1, "The Academic Setting."

Further, he expressed the feeling that if one did not have rules of confidentiality,

> the effects would be very, very open response of individuals to pressure... and perhaps not voting according to their conscience.... It would also be highly disruptive because... people have to work together in a collegial fashion; if the candidate is hired, then there is an immediate antagonism between him and all the people he knows voted against him; if the candidate is not hired, again the same kind of divisive activity takes place within the department.

He concluded that confidentiality is

> essential to academic freedom. It's very difficult to conceive that one can have a collegial university or preserve true academic freedom without confidentiality in the appointment, promotions or tenure process.

Members of the department echoed these views. Harold Waller, in an attempt to justify the absence of discussion at the departmental assembly that considered the Appointment Committee's recommendation of Mandel, took Freedman's argument even further.

> And now, if you are going to have an open discussion about it, then the voters are going to disclose their votes, and it is not going to be secret any more. So... having a complete discussion is, I think, contradictory [to the] notion of the secret ballot.

This rather bizarre view of a democratic process that had to take place in total silence was shared by Nayar.

> If we are going to have discussions, then it would undermine the secret ballot. That would be like voting generally; if people were to say why one votes for one candidate or another, then it won't be a secret ballot; that just applies to public office as it applies here.

Nayar explained the need for a secret ballot—to protect voters against illegitimate pressure from other members of the department. However, in putting forth this argument, he inadvertently admitted what everyone was so much at pains to deny—that illegitimate, non-academic criteria can and often do enter into academic decisions.

> We use a secret ballot so that nobody is under pressure or can be put under pressure to vote for one person or another, because, supposing there was a situation, some people, because of seniority or something else, had some leverage in the department. But I think there is really no such thing as leverage; we are all independent intellectuals in the department. But supposing there were. It is precisely to avoid a situation, that nobody can put pressure on anybody else, that we have the procedure of secret ballot.

The contradiction was blatant; if undue pressure was unthinkable among "independent intellectuals," why the need for such elaborate protection at the expense of an open discussion of the merits and shortcomings of the candidate? This raises the suspicion that the preoccupation with secrecy was perhaps not at all meant to safeguard the purity of the decision, but rather the "right" of the voter to apply *any* criteria he or she saw fit, "free" from outside scrutiny. Certainly one could interpret in this way the following statement by Waller: "If you are going to have a secret vote, then there is reason for the secret vote, and the secret vote is to protect the voter."

The vice-principal's arguments for respecting the secrecy of the vote did not survive cross-examination and confrontation with the reality of the university's functioning. For it was duly established that in the case of tenure decisions at McGill, everyone participating in the decision-making process knows how everyone else voted. Moreover, the candidates themselves receive a statement, or statements, from those who dissent from the majority opinion, and these are frequently signed. In other words, candidates, as well as the voters, will regularly know how each member of the department voted.

Presented with one such signed report from the Political Science Department, Freedman was at a loss for words. He had just finished explaining how the principle of confidentiality in university hiring and promotion was universally accepted in the

79

Western world. His initial reaction was to demand to know "how this confidential document came into his [Allen Fenichel's, the questioner] possession." Regaining his composure, he offered: "No procedures are perfect the first time they are put into effect, but the principle, we still maintain the principle, and that doesn't in any way alter our opinion that the principle should be upheld." The fact that this hallowed principle found no application in the real life of the university was no reason for its officials not to proclaim it. Was this also the case, perhaps, for the principle of academic freedom?

Caught red-faced in the contradiction between word and deed, the university was forced to drop this defence. On the day it was to appear before Superior Court, it informed the commission that it would not object to witnesses being questioned about their vote. When Mandel complained that McGill's hypocritical adherence to principle had caused a five-month delay in the hearing, McGill's lawyer retorted that the university had every right to change its mind. "Even on matters of principle?" asked Mandel. "Especially on matters of principle," came the reply.

We Didn't Reject Him—We Just Chose Someone Else

Faced with the necessity of revealing and, therefore, justifying their vote, the initial approach of virtually all the hostile witnesses was to deny voting against Mandel. Rather, they voted for other candidates. This, it was hoped, would spare them from the need to offer an explanation in terms of Mandel's academic credentials, which were strong. Any such explanation was bound to seem doubtful. (Indeed, this is what the various investigators concluded.) On the other hand, arguments in terms of "global judgement" and "needs of the department"—that were always established after the fact and had an uncanny ability to shift at a moment's notice—seemed unassailable.

Barbara Haskel offered the rather original analogy of being presented with four good things, and being asked:

> "chocolate, vanilla, strawberry or raspberry?" and you choose chocolate... and someone said "why not raspberry?".... Your preference is from the perception that you have of the needs

of the department.... I would really like to stress that, because, since you are dealing with good people, to say we choose "x" is not to say "y" is bad. I think that is so important... that we were dealing with very good people. In the current job market, one has excellent choices, and then it becomes a matter of taste in the sense of betting on where you want the field to go.

Kunz was more explicit in interpreting the department's feelings about Mandel: "I don't think there is a group of people who were opposing Dr. Mandel. You can say that a majority of the department preferred another candidate." Many were very open in their praise of Mandel's credentials—Stein, for example: "I had read... part of Dr. Mandel's manuscript which he had left in the department office and I thought very highly of it; I thought, really it was an excellent piece of work.... I don't think there is any question about the qualifications of Dr. Mandel as a scholar."

But this tactic, too, proved impossible to sustain. Mandel's name had been put before the department not once, but twice, as the *only* recommendation of the Appointments Committee. Logically, then, he had to be rejected, not simply ranked as one of the five qualified people. Moreover, this was the first time in more than ten years, during which many appointments had been made, that the Appointments Committee's recommendation had been rejected. In addition, both Canadian law and CAUT guidelines called for preference to qualified Canadians. If these were to be set aside, then it was only to be expected that an argument be made in terms of Mandel's credentials. Finally, those who argued that they voted against Mandel because they preferred another candidate had no way of being certain that the Appointments Committee would, in fact, recommend their preference. Mandel would have had to be at the bottom of everyone's list, a coincidence that clearly suggested a specific antipathy toward him.

As Waller put it in his typically unfortunate but very revealing formulation: "I don't know what is going to come out of the Appointments Committee next. You take your chances when you do that, but that's... that's... that's politics!" Waller had voted against Mandel because, he claimed, he preferred Bielasiak. But he ended up voting for Debardeleben.

Jerome Black's explanation for his vote against Mandel is even more suggestive.

> I agonized over my decision and ultimately voted no.... I agonized because he [Mandel] was the only Canadian candidate.... That concerned me a great deal... and I spent three or four days really debating that in my head but in the end I decided that another factor was more important to me and that factor was that I thought the department ought to have a much more contemporary empirical perspective or orientation.... I realize that's a narrow viewpoint.... This was a major factor that overruled my concern that we didn't have enough Canadians.

Black explained that Bielasiak, who was engaging in empirical methods, was his first choice. He also indicated that in his mind, Bielasiak had been effectively eliminated and the choice was between Mandel and Debardeleben. He voted for Debardeleben as his second choice.

When asked, "Is Debardeleben a quantitative specialist?" he responded, "No, not at all." He might have added that neither was she Canadian. Black, who would have wanted a quantitative specialist and a Canadian, rejected Mandel, a qualified Canadian, in favour of a candidate who was neither a quantitative specialist nor a Canadian. The illogic is blatant and points to other unspoken criteria that operated against Mandel.

Paul Noble's behaviour was even more revealing. When he gave his proxy to one of his colleagues, he gave no other indication for its use except that "it would be cast as a negative with respect to this particular motion [that Mandel be appointed] of the Appointments Committee." Noble leaves little doubt that he approved of everyone but Mandel. "I just felt there must be better candidates." He was unable to recall, however, if he had seen Mandel's curriculum vitae that year. He had not attended his talk nor that of three of the other candidates.

A friendly witness testified directly to the existence of active opposition to Mandel. Andrey Hollinger, a student representative on the Appointments Committee, observed that "there were a few members [of the Appointments Committee], but one that I personally know of, who... well, obviously did not want to appoint Mandel.... She [Haskel] just kept picking out other names.... The whole feeling was that they really didn't... want him."

The attempt by witnesses to convince the commission that their judgement was based on a simple choice among "goods" was a device to avoid having to offer academic reasons for their rejection of Mandel that could be subjected to close scrutiny (and therefore revealed to be invalid, as, in fact, was later done). It was a device that was no more successful than the self-serving defence of the secret ballot and absence of discussion. Under further questioning, there emerged more specific reasons for the rejection of Mandel's candidacy.

Well, If You Must Know...

Many of the witnesses took great pains to stress how important the appointment was, as the department had never before had a full-time position in Soviet and East European politics. According to Blema Steinberg, "everybody felt... strongly that this was an important decision and worked to participate in making it." But this claim contrasted with the flimsy and often trivial reasons offered for the vote against Mandel in terms of his qualifications. It became clear why the departmental meeting had avoided debate, or even discussion, of these qualifications.

To start with, Mandel had an excellent publications record and was, therefore, immune from attack in the area that is generally considered most important, and the least subjective, in evaluating academic performance. Witnesses therefore tended to minimize the importance of publications and to argue (as did Kunz, Stein, Waller, and others) that though Mandel was ahead (with two books and several articles) of Debardeleben in this area, Debardeleben, whose record was very much weaker, showed great promise as a scholar.

Many witnesses testified as to their doubts about Mandel's training, which was in sociology rather than political science, though not one could explain how this training adversely affected his teaching or research performance. Indeed, the Appointments

Committee had selected Mandel as the most qualified of some two dozen candidates and even the hostile witnesses had praised the quality of his scholarly achievements. Nevertheless, Waller, echoing the others, explained his vote for Debardeleben in these terms: "I thought she had better academic qualifications.... For one thing, her degree was in political science, which was very important." So important was this consideration, in fact, that no one had thought to raise it before that moment.

James Mallory, on the other hand, thought some saw an issue "in the marked preference of some of my colleagues for political scientists whose training and approach are more behavioural rather than historical." Yet Mallory, like Black, admitted that in this respect Mandel's orientation differed little from Debardeleben's.

The only witness to specifically mention Mandel's teaching performance as an issue was Black. As honours adviser, he claimed to have received some reports about "mediocre may be too strong a word, but far from exemplary teaching." But he admitted that these were only informal reports, "not a systematic sondage." He apparently thought so little of this that he never raised the issue of Mandel's teaching in the Appointments Committee. In fact, according to Black the only one to raise the issue was a student and she did so as an argument favouring Mandel's candidacy. Asked if the question had arisen, he replied: "I don't think by the faculty, but I think, I forget the name of the undergraduate student [representative], but she raised it and positively so. Certainly there was a very strong letter in Professor Mandel's file."

Unable to directly attack Mandel's teaching, several witnesses did express the view that he was a poor communicator. Thus Janice Stein felt that Mandel's talk "was not as effective to me as I would have liked.... Sometimes it is very difficult to make up your mind exclusively on the basis of one talk... but I had some major reservations." Although one talk was an insufficient basis for judgement, Stein did not make any further effort to learn about Mandel's teaching. Instead, she claimed her decision to reject Mandel was finally determined by an event of astonishing triviality, even for this Political Science Department.

> A second factor did weigh with me after the talk.... [My class] had a visitor, a journalist from Washington, who came to talk about the analysis of Soviet intention.... I asked Dr. Mandel to come to the seminar... He came but he didn't enter into the discussion even though I had some reservations about the analysis that was being offered.... And this was a matter of concern to me.... And that was the factor that made me choose the others over Dr. Mandel.

Thus, even though it was Stein who had reservations, Mandel is faulted for not raising these. Though she was supposedly very concerned, Stein admitted she did not bother to ask Mandel about this. Had she asked, he would have told her that as a guest in the class he felt he should defer to the students during the brief, fifteen-minute question period. Mandel had not been told that he was expected to perform. Yet it was enough to finally make her decide that his career at McGill should be ended.

A number of witnesses held it against Mandel that he failed to engage in social relations with them, seeing in this an intellectual defect of major importance. According to Kunz, "one thing that I heard on and off was that people felt that although Dr. Mandel had been in the department during that year, he had not really established a strong presence and that his was not really a very, sort of dynamic personality, and so on." Noble, who was on sabbatical and admitted to knowing virtually nothing about the candidates, "would go into the office occasionally and did have the occasional conversation.... David did seem to be a quiet person... and I certainly had some questions in my mind as to what extent he would communicate satisfactorily in classroom situations." Noble may have had questions, but, like Stein, he did not bother to seek answers. Nevertheless, he managed to decide that any of the short-listed candidates was better than Mandel. Nayar echoed the others:

> In the sense that Professor Mandel had been with the department a whole year, but there was no relationship to any of the other faculty members... [he was] alienated from the department, withdrawn from the department. There wasn't any cultivation of ties... and this might have been a factor in terms of what people will deduce from it as the kind of

relationship that a professor will establish with his colleagues and with students.

It was, of course, unthinkable that Mandel could have little to say to the powers-that-be in the McGill Political Science Department and still be a good scholar and teacher.

David Wootton, a visiting professor in the department from 1981 to 1983, put the issue in a more realistic perspective in his testimony.

> I was a bit surprised that people did not go out of their way to be friendly, but I interpreted it as partly due to the fact that I was passing through. Therefore, it was simpler to ignore me. So that I think the position of a visiting professor is a bit special. But I think one could distinguish between the way some visiting professors are treated and the way other visiting professors are treated. And I think that it does come down to questions of politics, culture, and so forth.

Andrey Hollinger, the undergraduate student representative on the Appointments Committee, was even clearer about what was truly at issue in the expressed concern over Mandel's "unsociability."

> There was a brief exchange [in the Appointments Committee], that Professor Mandel never... went to parties or went out to eat or had coffee with them.... The whole feeling was that they didn't really like him.... He didn't fit in with them.... It was obviously part of his personality. He was never with them. But part of his personality are the views he held.... If he believed what they believed, they could all sit together and have lunch or coffee.... There would have been no problem.... There was a maintenance strike.... Mandel cancelled his classes. He didn't want to cross the picket line.... It just shows how different they are, how they are on one extreme and he is on the other.

The CAUT committee of inquiry, for its part, found that the department was not known for its collegiality, in either the social or academic sense. Moreover, Mandel had established friendships and intellectual contacts with a part of the department as well as with people elsewhere at McGill and at other universities in Canada, the United States, and the United Kingdom.

When it came down to it, there were no academic reasons for the vote against Mandel. The chair of the Human Rights committee of inquiry acknowledged this when he put the following question to one of the witnesses:

> My problem is to really understand the situation. I think that Professor Mandel was a qualified candidate. I think everybody agreed on this. He had a good *scolarité*, publications and everything, and everybody came here and said, well, he had nothing against him. Maybe he was a little shy. And they all say, well, it's more in terms of preference for other candidates. And it is not clear to me that the other candidates were really superior in terms of qualifications. That is why I wonder if maybe, in your mind, when you have to make a choice, you exclude him before thinking of somebody else?

Indeed, it was clear that Mandel was not liked by most, if not all the more senior members of the department. Filippo Sabetti, in his remarkably cautious testimony—about the only thing he admitted to being certain of was his name—told of a phone call from Thomas Bruneau a few days before the departmental meeting: "He said, 'I don't like,' he probably might have said, 'I don't like Mandel'." This much was established. But did this dislike have anything to do with Mandel's politics? Certainly not!, chimed the chorus of hostile witnesses. It couldn't possibly have, since we didn't even know his politics!

Politics? We Didn't Know He Had Any!

In their zeal to deny any knowledge of Mandel's politics, witnesses contradicted themselves and each other and defied common sense. The list of those who pleaded ignorance is long, so we will limit ourselves to a few illustrations:

> Question: But you are saying you had no perception about his politics?
> Kunz: No, I didn't have any.

Question: Your knowledge of his politics was... zero?

Steinberg: Yes, that is right.

Stein: I don't know if he knew my views. I certainly had no idea of what his were.

Waller: My experience during that year was that he did not identify himself as anything. I had absolutely no clues as to what his views on anything were.... I never knew he took a position on anything. I wasn't aware he had any position.... I don't think anyone knew anything about Mandel's politics.

Some pressed this claim of "political innocence" beyond Mandel, in the apparent belief that consistency makes for credibility. Steinberg, Waller, Haskel, and Bruneau either denied knowing or could not state for certain whether Noumoff was a Marxist. These were people who had worked with Noumoff in the same department for fifteen years, a time during which Noumoff had been consistently and visibly active in the university on left-wing issues. Moreover, they had just finished reviewing his published work in connection with his request for tenure. Anyone with the least familiarity with university life, let alone the McGill Political Science Department, will recognize the incredible nature of these claims coming from trained specialists in political analysis.

However, a few witnesses were able to describe Mandel's politics without difficulty. Bornstein classified him as "a left-wing socialist with strong Trotskyist leanings." Asked if this was common knowledge in the department, he replied: "It's pretty clear to me that people knew that they were dealing with somebody way to the left of them." Black, who testified to having had extremely little contact with Mandel, based his answer on Mandel's seminar: "He was engaging in Marxist scholarship in portraying the Russian Revolution in ways, let us say, a pluralist wouldn't. I think that was clear." Noble, who, while on sabbatical, hardly saw Mandel, was left with the impression, after a conversation about Israel, that "he was a person critical of some Israeli policy."

But even those who pleaded total ignorance were forced to admit, under questioning, that this was not quite true. Thus, Waller conceded that "there were certain elements of a Marxist approach in the lecture that I heard. Yes." But he nimbly leapt over the contradiction by observing that one must "make a distinction between a Marxist in a political sense and a Marxist in an intellectual sense."

But not all witnesses were able to match this intellectual agility. Black, a hostile witness, stated: "I think the two travel together.... I can sense a relationship between Marxist scholarship and Marxist political beliefs, as I can that relationship between liberal-democratic political beliefs and liberal-democratic scholarship."

Yet it was Kunz who showed the most fertile imagination when it came to fine distinctions. He admitted that he had once observed in conversation that Mandel was having an identity crisis, that he was not sure whether he was a worker or a professor. But this, he insisted, was "not a political insight; it is an existential insight." But even the imaginative Kunz was forced to retreat when faced with testimony that Mandel had informed him, as chair of the department, that he was suspending classes during the maintenance workers' strike. After a fumbling effort to deny that this act had any political significance, Kunz "reinterpreted" his original testimony: "What I meant was that nobody talked to me about his politics." Yes, he did, after all, have some general idea of Mandel's politics, but offered: "I don't know the details of his political views."

Stein, too, backtracked, conceding that Mandel's manuscript examined "class factors" and that he "has a point of view on which he formed the whole analysis."

Did Bruneau and Sabetti, despite their firm denials, also perhaps have "general ideas" about Mandel's politics? We have only a peculiar bit of testimony from Sabetti concerning the context of Bruneau's phone call: "He might have wanted to say that [I should vote against Mandel because he is a Marxist], but he didn't." Why Bruneau "might have wanted to say that" and why Sabetti might have thought that Bruneau "might have wanted to say that"—when neither had the least inkling at the time that Mandel was in fact a Marxist—will have to remain a puzzle.

Politics in a Political Science Department? Who Ever Heard of Such Nonsense!

When the claim that they had nothing against Mandel and merely preferred another proved untenable; when they failed to justify their rejection of Mandel on academic grounds; and when their defence of ignorance of Mandel's politics was revealed to be full of holes, there logically remained only one tactic: to argue that, despite everything, the Mandel decision could not have involved political bias, because the members of the McGill Political Science Department are much too professional to allow politics to enter into academic matters. But here, too, contradictions abounded.

Waller, for one, was unequivocal about how easy it was to separate strong feelings about political matters from considerations of an academic nature. Responding to one question, he boldly asserted that he would even hire a Nazi if he was qualified for the job: "I am a strong civil libertarian.... Although I find Naziism repugnant, I would not take a person's political beliefs into account when being asked to state in a tenure setting, whether someone should be appointed or not."

Haskel seconded this claim, describing a degree of compartmentalization of her colleagues' psyches rarely (if ever) observed in sane people: "They are individuals who have a strong interest in their area. Their political attitudes... are their own. That is their private life. I don't think that bears on our department in any way. That is not what is brought... into discussion of the suitability or unsuitability of candidates.... That would be considered terribly illegitimate." But further probing from the investigator forced her to modify this tidy picture: "There is no guarantee with human beings that there isn't bias.... In the department we have different views. And there is some check and balance in the sense that there are people who feel quite strongly on the opposite sides of the questions."

Nayar also adopted this more moderate position, testifying that in the Noumoff tenure decision, the latter's politics— "Marxist, radical, anti-Zionist"—were indeed of interest to his colleagues. "For example, his position was discussed in the tenure committee."

However, he hastened to add that "people are not carried away by these views to oppose him." But, on further reflection, he wasn't sure of this: "I have a hard time trying to figure out my motive as an individual.... How can I figure out other people's motives?"

Kunz had the same problem: "...even in situations in which I personally disagree with people... I never come away with the conviction that the other side acted out of political motivation." On the other hand, he, too, had to admit that it was hard to be sure:

> Very often people may not admit it to themselves.... [Academic reasons] could be rationalizations of real motives.... You have to be a mind reader to really know.... I don't have proof that people acted out of political motivation. It is possible that people have a mixture of motives.

Dean Vogel, who had spent ten years in that post, admitted to seeing his share of unprofessional conduct. But in every case in which the accusation of political bias had been raised, he had found the issue to be really a conflict of personalities. However, when pressed, he, too, yielded: "I think that, like all considerations that enter into this process, it [politics] is a consideration within limits."

Bruneau also tried to reduce it all to a question of personality. He explained the avoidance of discussion of Mandel's qualifications, at the departmental meeting, in these terms:

> [In academia] maybe more than in other places, the personalities of people have full flexibility, and all kinds of little foibles and quirks seem to come out and people interpret things in a very personal way and attach on them or attach on their friends' personalities in various ways. So, discussion would get into something that relates to a person's personality [and] tend to become extremely heated.

Bruneau did not clarify why a discussion of qualifications would degenerate into a heated exchange over personality. Certainly, this would make more sense if in place of "personality" one read "politics."

This heretical thought was offered by Hollinger. As an undergraduate student in political science, her socialization into professional ethics was obviously still incomplete. When asked if personality was important in the decision against Mandel, she replied, "but part of his personality are the views he expressed.... That is part of a person.... If he believed what they believed, they would all sit... together. There would have been no problem."

Some members of the department had little trouble recognizing the strongly politicized nature of the department. When asked about the role of political views on the Middle East, Mallory stated: "Some of my colleagues are not only strongly involved in this but they are deeply committed, but from time to time this affects their attitudes on particular issues." Noumoff was even clearer:

> If I were a political scientist looking... from the outside... I would certainly say that there are people who share a definite and clear and well-known [view on a] set of issues, and it is only reasonable that they would try to give expression to that perception of the world.... I think it is not unreasonable to suggest that the Middle East question is a very strong question of concern.

Wootton, a visitor in the department, offered this political analysis of the department:

> It would put great weight upon... the way proxy votes are used. I was very struck recently to discover that Professor Brecher is away and Professor Steinberg has his proxy vote to use in any circumstance, on any matter, as she chooses. I would take that to be evidence of the existence of a party in most political contexts because it seems to me to be a matter of a party alliance.... I don't think the department is entirely divided along two lines but I think a fairly small group of people who vote consistently together and who organize their votes are able to have quite an important effect on decisions within the department.

But, of course, as Professor Waller had offered, "that's politics!"

Samuel Freedman, vice-principal academic and official spokesman at the hearing for McGill's collegial ideology, in his enthusiastic defence of secrecy, gave perhaps the most realistic description of how McGill University (and not only McGill) actually functions:

> There are often ideological or scientific differences of opinion within a department.... There could be pressure from within the department, there can be pressure from deans, or even, I regret to say it, university administrations. That's a conceivable matter. There can be pressure from the business community or sources of private funding of the university.

Politics in a political science department? Indeed!

4 The Report

The CAUT fact-finding committee issued its final report in October 1982 after considering written commentaries by interested parties on its preliminary report of March 1982. The report of the investigation for the Québec Human Rights Commission (HRC) was released to Mandel and to McGill in January 1983. Its conclusions, based on much more extensive inquiry (more than fifty hours of testimony), both complemented and reinforced those of the first report.

What follows is a summary of the main points of the two reports, which together ran for more than 250 pages.

Canadianization

The CAUT report began by noting:

Dr. Mandel is, by all accounts, an outstanding young Canadian professor of political science. He specializes in Soviet and Eastern European political systems. He is fluent in English, French and Russian. We are neither authorized nor qualified to evaluate his scholarship. We could not avoid being impressed, however, by the uniformity of the opinions expressed

95

by his former colleagues—including several who dispute his allegations of bias and impropriety—to the effect that his scholarly accomplishments are remarkable for one at his early career stage.

And it went on to affirm:

> Dr. Mandel is a Canadian; the person appointed is not. Although McGill University appears to have satisfied both federal and provincial authorities that it complied in this case with the minimum requirements of the law, it did not comply with CAUT's *Guidelines on Canadianization and the University*....
>
> ...Moreover, quite apart from the text of the CAUT Guidelines, there does not appear to have been any significant consideration of the "Canadianization" issue at any decision stage in connection with the determination not to appoint Dr. Mandel. There was some discussion of the issue by the departmental Appointments Committee, though even that discussion seems to have been desultory. The issue was not discussed at the Department meeting that rejected the Committee's first recommendation, and there was no indication from the discussions we had with members of the Department and with senior administrators that the question was ever given serious consideration by them in arriving at their respective decisions.
>
> Subsequently, at the suggestion of CAUT, McGill University has given consideration to the "Canadianization" question, and has now adopted a new position based upon recommendations of MAUT.... However, it still fails to accept the CAUT Guidelines, quoted above, that were ignored in the Mandel case. There appears, therefore, to be a firm and conscious rejection on the part of McGill University of these two crucial elements of the CAUT Canadianization Guidelines.

The committee also rejected the argument that observance of the guidelines would not necessarily have led to Mandel's appointment: "There is no evidence that the Department regarded any other Canadian applicant as better qualified than Dr. Mandel. The Appointments Committee clearly did not."

The HRC inquiry was not directly concerned with the immigration law or with "Canadianization" as such. The investigator's report, however, does confirm this conclusion of the CAUT report.

Only one professor, Jerome Black, paid any attention at all to the "Canadianization" issue, and when it came to the voting, he discarded it as a consideration:

> What seems curious to me [wrote the Québec Human Rights investigator] in this reasoning is that he first chooses Mandel because he gives priority to the "Canadian" criterion; he then changes his mind after much reflection, not to say agonizing, because he decides that the criterion of "empirical methodology," according to his perception of the department's needs, should have priority over "Canadianization": and he, therefore, chooses Debardeleben, who "was not skilled in empirical methodology." It is as if he then completely forgot this criterion of "Canadianization," which he nevertheless considered so important and which normally should have intervened in his choice between Mandel and Debardeleben, since the latter is an American and neither of the two answers to the priority criterion which he had finally fixed for himself in choosing Bielasiak.

The report also indicates that the department chair supplied misleading information to the immigration authorities, who undertook two rather perfunctory inquiries into Mandel's complaint. They were told that Mandel had been rejected because his Ph.D. was in sociology rather than political science, although, in the testimony before CAUT, this reason was mentioned by only one witness, and as one reason among others. In addition, the authorities were told that Mandel had been selected by a narrow margin in the Appointments Committee and that the candidate ultimately appointed had been its second choice. In fact, the vote in the Appointments Committee was 5 v. 3, while in the department as a whole, Mandel had at the outset a simple majority of at least ten supporters, which, according to testimony, was more than twice as many as any other short-listed candidate. Moreover, "in actual fact, the Appointments Committee had not fixed a second choice, and the candidate appointed was very much a compromise candidate with little initial support."

Procedural Defects

Both reports agreed that the procedures actually followed were inconsistent with the justifications offered for their existence and that they resulted in injury to Mandel.

Absence of Open Discussion

According to the CAUT report,

> the first questionable practice concerns the nature of the Department meeting. Dr. Mandel complains that most faculty members had already made up their minds before coming to the meeting. Most of those with whom we discussed the matter agreed with Dr. Mandel on this point, whether or not they supported his contentions in general. There had been a period of quite intense individual and small group discussion among the faculty members prior to the Deparment meeting, and these discussions appear to have been decisive in shaping the opinions of several members of the Department. It was hardly surprising, therefore, that the debate which took place during the Department meeting was brief and shallow. There is nothing wrong with informal preliminary discussions among persons who are called upon to render formal decisions. Where, however, as in this case, the preliminary discussions appear to have been conclusive, the value of holding a departmental "meeting" on the question is lost. The major advantage of a general meeting is the opportunity it provides for the decision-makers to take account of all points of view, and to have those which they tentatively favour tested by unrestricted debate. While this is by no means the only valid method of arriving at decisions, it has advantages which no other technique has. Those advantages are lost when the "meeting" becomes little more than an occasion for registering votes.

Similarly, the HRC investigation noted:

> All the discussions seem to have taken place in the corridors, and the Departmental Assembly was merely an occasion for registering the vote—all this under the veil of the rule of

confidentiality only more or less respected in a department that in the final analysis finds its raison d'être in politics.

One really must admit that in such a context anything is possible.

Both investigations questioned the logic and consistency of the justifications offered for the secrecy. The CAUT committee found that

> the secretiveness of the process was defended by many members of the Department on the grounds that frank statements of non-support for a particular candidate could result in poor future relations between the candidate, if appointed, and the critical faculty members. While this may be true, several other factors should be borne in mind. One is the loss of the benefits of full and searching discussion, referred to above. Another is the fact that most faculty members appear to have been willing to engage in full discussion, in small groups, among their faculty colleagues.

Similarly, the Human Rights report states:

> One puts much emphasis on the principle of confidentiality and secrecy of the vote, while in practice many will admit that everything gets known in very little time.
>
> There indeed seems to be an entire world between what is said and the everyday practice....
>
> ...Thus, several witnesses testified that their preference was known even though they had not participated in any lobbying. Others said they knew that such-and-such candidate would meet with much opposition from certain colleagues and that another candidate was more "acceptable." In this context, it becomes an open secret.

Moreover, the HRC investigation found that Frank Kunz, as chair of both the department and the Appointments Committee, had acted to effectively preclude discussion of Mandel's qualifications:

> The most troubling procedural incident, apart from the entire question of the absence of discussion, remains the ambiguous role of Chairman Kunz, who rejected a decision

[of the Appointments Committee, to present Mandel's name a second time to the Departmental Assembly] in which he had earlier participated.[1]

This seems important to me because his decision on a point of procedure had the direct consequence of definitively excluding David Mandel and of propelling forth the candidacy of Debardeleben, who was "his own" candidate.

In taking this decision, there was a very great probability that the Appointments Committee would return with a recommendation in favour of the latter, since it was known that by that time half of the members of the Appointments Committee were in favour of her.

Since this decision was approved by a majority vote of the assembly, one could see in this a very indirect way for the assembly to propose a candidate itself.[2]

[Prof. Kunz] explains that to return a second time with the same candidate made no sense, since the assembly would have had to begin anew "ad vitam eternam".... One can permit oneself to think that, all the same, he could have thought of that beforehand....

...In reality, what the Appointments Committee meant in thus returning with the same candidate after having thought everything through again was to provoke discussion about the initial recommendation, which it felt to have been rejected without sufficient indication as to the type of candidate that was being sought.

Prof. Kunz must have known this, and his decision, therefore, had the effect of preventing any other discussion.

Proxy Voting

Both reports cited the use of proxy votes in the department meeting as an important procedural shortcoming. The CAUT report observed that it reinforced the impression that the department attached little importance to the meeting. The HRC investigation, citing the testimony of Professor Paul Noble, went further to cast doubts on the motivation behind the proxy vote.

---

[1] Kunz had agreed to this procedure while in the Appointments Committee, but when challenged by a member of the Departmental Assembly, he ruled the procedure out of order and was supported in this by a majority of the assembly.
[2] The constitution stipulates that the Departmental Assembly can only accept or reject a candidate; it cannot itself propose.

Noble... was on sabbatical during this period and... gave his proxy to Kunz or Nayar without any other instruction except to vote against the [Appointments Committee's] recommendation.

What is curious in this case is that, although he had not really participated in the discussions of the period... and although he clearly did not know much about the other candidates (he claims to have gone to one of the talks), he explains his opposition with the same arguments as those given by certain professors, i.e. his [Mandel's] too historical approach, his Ph.D. in sociology, his shy personality, as well as his own profound conviction that there were stronger candidates than Mandel.... His memory is feeble and his explanations are tortuous, so that one can think that he had harvested all the reasons invoked [by others], without really being capable of justifying them on the basis of his own experience.

Access to Confidential Information

The CAUT report made the following criticism:

Another irregularity in the procedure employed by the Department relates to access to confidential information about candidates. Whereas all members of the Appointments Committee, including student members, have access to all information received, whether or not of a confidential nature, other members of the Department have a right to access to non-confidential material only. This is strange. If the full Department has the power to review and reverse recommendations of the Appointments Committee, it should surely be given access to the same information upon which the Committee based its recommendations. The procedure adopted means that the review body is less well-equipped to determine the matter than the group whose recommendation is being reviewed.... Those who review appointment recommendations must have access to all the information available to those who made the original recommendations.

In this context, the HRC investigator was disturbed by Kunz's failure to explain the reasons behind the Appointments Committee's recommendation of Mandel.

One can think that this way of proceeding contravened the spirit of the department's constitution or, at least, a certain custom or practice that had developed over the years since the constitution was adopted.

Otherwise, the system makes no sense and one can find no logic in it. If the very basis of the system is that only the elected Appointments Committee, which has access to all the information, can propose a candidate to the departmental assembly, which does not have access to this information and which has only the right to veto, then it seems implicit to me that there should be a presentation of the recommended candidate that includes an explanation for the recommendation and a discussion or an exchange of information, especially in a context where the recommendation was not unanimous, in order that the body that exercises the decision-making power be able to make an enlightened decision.

The Constitution of the Department [states the following]: "The Appointments Committee shall examine and consider the applications for new appointments and shall report to each regular meeting of the section."

It is not very explicit, but one can think that the use of the word "report" implies a certain justification of the recommendation and not simply the name of the selected candidate.

To think otherwise, qualifying this manner of proceeding as regular and justifying it by the fact that the vote is secret, negates the very idea of making a report to the assembly, since the latter becomes in such a context merely an occasion for registering the vote. The upshot of this would be that the body that makes the decision deprives itself of an instrument whose very raison d'être is to allow it to better exercise its decision-making power.

Moreover, one cannot help but see a connection between those who defend this interpretation of the procedure and the group of professors whom the plaintiff is implicating, as they are, after all, the same people.

Failure to Give Reasons

The department's refusal to give Mandel an explanation for its decision was also cited by CAUT as a major procedural defect, although it noted that the nature of the procedures themselves—the absence of discussion at the departmental meeting and the secret ballot—made it virtually impossible to arrive at a "departmental reason" or reasons.

> Most important of all, had the Department meeting agreed on reasons for the decision, and had those reasons been communicated to Dr. Mandel, he would have had an opportunity to refute any reasons he regarded as improper or unsubstantiated before the decision was confirmed by higher authorities in the University. Procedures which deprived Dr. Mandel of these various opportunities to ensure against error in the appointment process must, in our opinion, be regarded as "unfair."

Political Bias

The secretive nature of the procedures adopted by the department made the investigation into the allegation of political bias even more difficult than it normally would have been in an appointments situation. The CAUT committee observed that "the department chose to adopt procedures which not only kept the reasons from the candidate, but also precluded their discovery by anyone else." Similarly, the author of the report for the Human Rights Commission noted that

> there emerges a firm will not to discuss openly the reasons for the choice. I find this troubling in the context of the allegations of the plantiff....
>
> The problem raised by the allegations of the plaintiff is particularly complex, on the one hand, because of the nature of the decision-making procedures—a collective decision made under the cover of a secret vote that reversed another collective decision taken also by a secret vote—and, on the other hand, because of the absence of defined criteria at the start, which would have allowed, up to a point, the exercise

of rational choice and the logical verification of it after the fact.

The CAUT committee noted a "remarkable uniformity" in the comments of a majority of professors with whom they spoke, who insisted that Mandel's politics could have played no role in their decision or that of most of their colleagues.

> This may have been the product of the Department meeting at which faculty members discussed the approach that should be taken to our inquiry. Consultations with the University's solicitor may also have contributed to the similarity of views expressed by the group. Consistency of expression by those who deny political bias does not constitute proof of its existence, however.
>
> If the decision was not based on political bias, as Dr. Mandel suggests, what were the reasons for it? While it is never possible to determine conclusively the reasons motivating a group of persons voting on a secret ballot, it is possible to examine the reasons advanced after the event by those involved in the decision, and to inquire whether they constitute plausible alternative explanations to the one alleged by Dr. Mandel.
>
> Three major alternative explanations for the decision were offered, two of which seem quite implausible.

One of these was the explanation originally offered by Kunz, that Mandel's "primary research interest was historical in nature and that a majority... favoured a more contemporary focus." This was found implausible for several reasons: no reference was made to a current focus in the job advertisement, Mandel "has also written and taught about current events," and, finally, very few of those interviewed mentioned it as a basis for the decision and "none place much emphasis on it."

The second reason was Mandel's Ph.D. in sociology. This, too, was rejected for several reasons: it had never been mentioned to Mandel nor did the nature of the Ph.D. appear in the ad; sociology and political science overlap (according to the university's own brochure) and Mandel's Ph.D. thesis was certainly on a political theme; and, again, few of those interviewed even mentioned this as a factor.

On the other hand, many people commented on Mandel's shyness, at least outside of the classroom, which prevented his developing satisfactory social relations with his colleagues. "They told us (again with striking conformity of expression)," said the CAUT report, "that the Department prizes 'collegial discourse'."

But this explanation also had to be rejected. First, "incompatibility" was an improper reason, according to CAUT guidelines. But in any case, "our discussions... led us to conclude... that the 'collegiality' of the Department is not as high, in either the social or academic sense, as it was represented to be.... Moreover, we are not persuaded that Dr. Mandel lacks the capacity for good collegial relations. We were told that he established cordial and intellectually stimulating relationships with a number of persons within the Department and in related departments. There is also evidence that he got along well with colleagues in other universities with which he was associated before coming to McGill."

> In other words, of the three reasons mentioned by those who made the decision, two seem implausible to us, and the third, while somewhat more likely, is unconvincing, and is in any event an improper basis for determining academic appointments.
>
> To what conclusion should this lead us about the propriety of the motivation for the decision not to appoint Dr. Mandel? If we were an adjudicative body, and if the onus of proof lay entirely on the shoulders of those seeking to impugn the decision, we would have to return a verdict of "not proven." Although a tribunal or investigative body with powers of subpoena might be able to turn up more compelling evidence, we have seen no conclusive proof that the appointment was denied for political or other improper reasons. However, we are not persuaded that the burden of proof should always lie with the professor in such matters. As we explained in Part I, the burden of proof ought to lie on the University where it has exclusive access to the reasons for an appointment decision and has failed to communicate those reasons to an unsuccessful applicant, and where known facts lead to a reasonable inference that the reasons were improper.
>
> Since those circumstances prevail in the present case, the burden of persuasion ought to be with McGill University.

Dr. Mandel was, as we have said, entitled to know the reason for not being appointed. The Department of Political Science, which was completely in control of the situation, chose to adopt procedures which not only kept the reasons from the candidate, but also precluded their discovery by those who took part in the decision. The most plausible is both unconvincing and improper, and the other two are no more probable, perhaps less so, than the improper reason suggested by Dr. Mandel and his supporters. Does not fairness dictate that Dr. Mandel be given the benefit of the doubt?

The committee answered in the affirmative, concluding:

Although we encountered no compelling proof supporting the charge of political bias, the Department, upon which the burden of explanation ought fairly to lie in the circumstances, has failed to persuade us that political bias was not a factor. The only alternative explanation that seems equally plausible is improper.

The HRC report, based on a much more thorough inquiry, reached the same conclusion but was able to formulate it in a more direct manner:

The general impression one gets from several of the testimonies heard in the course of the inquiry is that of the existence of a "party line."

What I mean by "party line," for lack of a better term, is the attitude of certain witnesses (Sabetti, Noble, Black) to justify their behaviour by the same arguments, which, however, they are able to articulate only very poorly in terms of their own personal frames of reference and logic. Indeed, these are the very same arguments that other witnesses developed in a more sustained and harmonious fashion.

One has the very strong impression that one group harvested the arguments of the other, clearly without taking them up in a coherent manner, as if lining themselves up on one side of the debate for one reason or the other.

He also noted the shifting nature of explanations that changed to fit the circumstances:

While at first, in view of the recommendation in favour of Mandel, they justify their choice in terms of the merits they find in other candidates, who respond more to a personal perception of the needs of the department; later, when faced with the candidacy of Debardeleben, there is a certain tendency to forget this perception of the needs of the department and to justify the choice in terms of what is held against Mandel.

[Furthermore, the claim that] they had no knowledge of Mandel's political convictions... seems very suspect to me, coming from specialists in political science.... Several made it to begin with but ended by admitting that, all the same, they had a certain perception.... Some were so categorical that one cannot help but be even more doubtful about this part of their testimony.

The investigator, in evaluating the explanations offered by the witnesses who voted against Mandel, arrived at conclusions very much in accord with those of the CAUT committee:

We easily share this evaluation of the relative merit of the explanations adduced by certain members of the department. At the same time, we tend to attribute more importance to the third ["non-collegiality"] in light of the testimonies we have heard....

One would believe that the respective "personalities" of the two candidates... was rather the determining factor. This is quite plausible, but this "personality" factor has as its corollary that of "compatibility" (with other people) and this *includes*, in the light of the highly politicized context of the Department of Political Science, the real or simply perceived political element.

The testimony on voting intentions indicated that Debardeleben had initially "garnered only a weak minority of votes," whereas the "ten easily identifiable votes" for Mandel[3] represented at least twice the support of any other candidate.

But what explains the phenomenon of the shift of the simple majority in favour of Mandel to an absolute majority in

---

[3] The actual vote for Mandel was nine, with Hollinger, a student representative who was absent from the assembly because of a death in her family, making ten.

favour of Debardeleben, who emerges as a compromise candidate? This is, of course, the normal consequence of the existing decision-making procedure. The system imposes a compromise once a recommendation fails to gather the majority of votes....

On the other hand, considering that it had become almost a custom that the recommendation of the Appointments Committee carries (one exception in 12 years), it became necessary in these circumstances for those opposed to Mandel to bring into being a certain "coalition" or, at least, to make sure that "the vote came out."

The evidence in this respect (lobbying) seems conclusive.

But this did not fully explain the outcome. In the opinion of the investigator, there existed another factor "which has a political content in the full sense of the term, more subtle and less perceptible, which allows one to explain in a plausible fashion the results of the procedure."

It seems to me that there exists a contradiction that speaks for itself.

That which they fault in Mandel, as regards his background, is found equally in Debardeleben, with a few differences of nuance (the somewhat more contemporary aspect of her research).

Proceeding from there, what is there to distinguish the two candidates, if not the fact that one refuses to admit?

Both have an academic background that is similar, in comparison with what they claimed to have wanted for the department in choosing other candidates (Sochor and Bielasiak).

Both have political orientations that go in the same direction, the difference being that Mandel had the opportunity to make these known, among other things, by participating in a picket line....

Thus, Mandel appeared more "to the left" than Debardeleben and it is for that reason that the latter represented a choice (a compromise choice) who was more acceptable for the group of professors....

In conclusion, "there were in this particular case political elements in the full sense of the term that intervened in the collective decision of the Department of Political Science to reject the candidacy of David Mandel, and in these circumstances, the complaint appears to us to be founded."

Remedy

It was part of the mandate of the CAUT committee of inquiry to suggest appropriate remedy. The proposal had four points:

1. The portions of this Report pertaining to Dr. Mandel should be made public by the University or by CAUT in the hope of partially remedying damage to Dr. Mandel's reputation caused by his unfair treatment.
2. A formal acknowledgement by the University that Dr. Mandel was treated unfairly would also help to rehabilitate his reputation, but not if couched in grudging language.
3a. A suitable remedy (but only if acceptable to Dr. Mandel) would be re-assessment for appointment to the same Department by a special external assessment committee, and subsequent appointment if successful.
3b. Alternatively, Dr. Mandel should be offered a visiting appointment in the Department, for one year with the option of an extension for a further year.
4. The University should, in any event, compensate Dr. Mandel for the financial losses stemming from his unfair treatment.

(The Committee, in fulfillment of the second of its mandates, also made general recommendations for guidelines on appointments. These appear in Appendix I.)

By the fall of 1982 there were two independent reports upholding David Mandel's charges against McGill's Political Science Department. Four neutral and independent people who interviewed the participants first-hand and sifted through the available evidence were unanimous in their conclusions that the allegations were founded. However, the report of the Human Rights inquiry was overturned by the Commission in a resolution passed on November 18, 1982, stating that "the inquiry does not reveal facts sufficiently serious, precise and coherent, capable of creating a presumption (*présomption*) of fact in favour of the plantiff..."[4] The Commission chair explained to Mandel that this decision was taken with a view to the probability of winning in a court of law.[5]

In their report, the CAUT committee had commented:

> The law of the land... offers a certain measure of protection against the more common forms of discrimination, and this protection applies to university professors as well as to others. But compliance with the minimum requirements of the law is not enough, especially in the case of universities, where academic freedom can be threatened by much subtler forms of discrimination than those the law proscribes.

The very length and intricacy of the HRC investigator's report pointed to the difficulties involved in dealing with discrimination in academic appointments cases within the narrow limits of the existing law. The president of the Human Rights Commission and the author of the report were both unable to cite a single complaint of discrimination in academic hiring which the Commission had succeeded in winning for the plaintiff.

Unless the CAUT board acted on the report of its fact-finding committee, an entire category of academics—the most vulnerable—would be left without protection.

---

[4] "L'enquête ne révèle pas de faits suffisamment graves, précis et concordants, susceptibles de créer une présomption de fait en faveur du plaignant..."
[5] See Chapter 6 for a discussion of the decision and how it was taken.

5 Implementing the Gibson Report: Three Strikes and You're Out

Mandel was now into the third year since his last full-time academic job. He continued teaching as *chargé de cours* at UQAM and occasionally at the Université de Montréal. He was also carrying on his work as part-time researcher for the Labour Studies Group at McGill's Centre for Developing-Area Studies (CDAS). His case before CAUT continued to take up a considerable amount of his time—although by now it had almost become a way of life. With the CAUT report, however, and the supporting conclusions of the Human Rights inquiry, it looked like all the effort was finally going to bear fruit.

The First Blow

The CAUT board was scheduled to meet at the end of October 1982. The report of its fact-finding committee was prominent on the agenda. But CAUT's Academic Freedom and Tenure Committee (AF&T) decided to recommend to the board that no action be taken on the report at the meeting. It soon

111

became clear that the majority of the AF&T committee were critical of the Gibson report and its recommendations. More than that, they had been, and continued to be, opposed to the very idea of an inquiry: as they were to observe in their "report" on the Gibson report, "the charge of political discrimination is by its nature virtually impossible to prove." For the present, they were satisfied to argue that it would be opportune to await the conclusions of the Québec Human Rights Commission (released only after the board meeting). Upon learning that the board was to hear a recommendation by the AF&T committee, Mandel asked to appear before the board, where he read the following statement:

> It has been two and a half years since I first brought this grievance before the CAUT.... Surely the time has come to finally draw a line and declare that any further delay is unconscionable and unbecoming of a body established to defend the interests of its members and to uphold what is best in Canada's academic traditions.
>
> All the more so as there is no valid reason to delay further. You have before you a strong, unanimous report, written by a committee of the highest calibre and reaffirmed without any significant change in the face of McGill's rebuttal.... Regarding my allegations of bias, it found that in this case the burden of proof should be shifted to the university, which was unable to disprove that the decision had not involved improper motive. This it could have done very simply—by offering a plausible legitimate reason for the rejection of my candidacy.... Discrimination is condemned by the academic community as well as society at large, and it is therefore extremely rare that it is exercised in an open manner that would yield direct types of proof. I submit that if the board rejects the Committee's conclusions in this area, it will for all practical purposes have renounced acting in cases involving discrimination.
>
> The AF&T has suggested that it would be opportune to await the conclusions of the Québec Human Rights Commission. This inquiry is a separate one. In establishing its own committee of inquiry, the board rejected McGill's argument that the Human Rights Commission investigation rendered unnecessary one by the CAUT. The issues examined

by the two inquiries are different and the types of proof they seek not necessarily of the same nature. The board has an inescapable responsibility to act independently on the report of a committee that it itself established. To wait for the findings of another inquiry would be an admission that the CAUT's procedures are without real meaning.

But the board accepted the AF&T committee's recommendation to postpone a decision. The meeting itself was characterized by a number of disturbing procedural irregularities. In a letter to Kenneth McGovern, president of CAUT, Mandel expressed his anger with the board's handling of the report:

> It must be clear to the board that in this case the Academic Freedom and Tenure Committee cannot be considered a neutral body. You will recall that in establishing the inquiry the board overruled the committee, which had rejected my request for a unilateral inquiry in the face of McGill's persistent refusal to co-operate. It would seem highly irregular that a body that opposed the very establishment of the inquiry should then be allowed to serve in an advisory capacity to the board on the report that resulted from the inquiry and, in that way, to have a decisive influence on the board's decision regarding that report.
>
> ...Even more disturbing is the fact that the Academic Freedom and Tenure Committee, which has no formal connection with the report, was allowed to voice an opinion on the report even before the members of the board themselves (so Dr. Sim tells me) could have a chance to discuss it—or, as seems the case, to even read it....
>
> It is very troubling to me that, had I not chanced to ask to speak before the board, a situation would have resulted in which two interested bodies, neither of which has any direct connection with the report (the other body is the MAUT, to which I shall come presently) would have been allowed to express their negative evaluations of the report, with no one there to speak for it. As a result, I was effectively deprived of counsel in what turned out to be a hearing. I appreciate that in a formal sense the decision was postponed. But in the meantime, I had no means of dealing on an equal footing with two highly prejudicial interventions that had been prepared in advance....

...The very presence of the representatives of the MAUT, one of the CAUT's largest constituent organizations, who were clearly there not to support the report, could only be prejudicial to the outcome of any discussion.

Ostensibly, the MAUT was there to speak to the procedures.... In fact, as you know, the MAUT's three representatives did not speak to the procedures. Virtually all their alloted time—and it was substantial—was devoted to an attack on the substance of the report. This was so even after someone finally instructed them to stick to the procedural question. And I repeat: the MAUT is not a party to the dispute; nor is it neutral—it has fought tooth and nail alongside the university administration to prevent my appeal.

If I found the above irregular and prejudicial, I was still in no way prepared for Dr. Handa's [president of MAUT] slanderous remarks against the Fact-Finding Committee itself. You will recall that Dr. Handa implied very clearly that the board had before it a biased report. In seeking possible sources of his bias, Dr. Handa proposed two that I can recall (but which you can verify from the minutes): that Dr. Gibson had once served together with Dr. Weldon[1] on a committee and that some members of the Fact-Finding Committee were pro-union, while "collegiality" is the ruling ideology at McGill....

I finally come to the board's decision to postpone any decision on the report. As I told the board in my statement, this is both cruel and uncalled for. The report, with only the most minor changes, has been in the hands of the CAUT for five months....

These are very grave matters. I left the board meeting with the clear sense that the report had not been treated fairly. I cannot help but wonder whether the recommendations of any report conducted in the real academic world into similar allegations would have a chance of being acted upon effectively. I also wonder how the board can now impartially evaluate the report, given what took place at the meeting.

The board was not moved. In a press release dated November 3, 1982, they commented that they had deferred action on the

---

[1] Jack Weldon advised Mandel on his case.

Gibson report until their March 1983 meeting in order to provide an opportunity for the AF&T committee to make its views known to the board.

The AF&T committee defended itself to Mandel in a letter from Professor J.K. Hiller, its chair. Hiller, who had often expressed his sympathy with Mandel's position, was unable or unwilling to impose his views on his committee:

> The Academic Freedom and Tenure Committee which met in August and October to discuss the report, was, with two exceptions, completely changed in personnel from the committee which rejected your original request. Members had none of the previous correspondence, and had only the Gibson report before them. In any event, the Committee is guided by strength of evidence and argument. Had the report been sufficiently persuasive, members would not have felt bound by the opinions of their predecessors.
>
> ...The preliminary view of the Committee is that although you may have been the victim of discrimination the Gibson report does not make a persuasive case for this. The investigators may well have seen and heard evidence that led them to the conclusion that something improper had occurred; if they did, that evidence is not in the report. Without a stronger case, we can hardly argue the reverse onus line with the McGill authorities. Secondly, the Committee did not find the criticisms of departmental procedures immediately convincing. Thirdly, the Committee is not yet ready to address what is in fact the complex issue of Canadianization. Hence my question to the Board: is the fact that a university has chosen, by its customary processes, to reject parts of the CAUT guidelines of itself sufficient ground for intervention? Fourthly, the Committee found the suggestions on proper hiring procedures controversial....
>
> I have to agree with you that the proceedings at the Board were unfortunate. However, I would argue that your points were well made and made an impression on the Board.... Indeed members evinced a great deal of sympathy for you in discussion, and cast about for some way in which assistance could be offered. There was no secret about MAUT's intention to address the Board, and I find it hard to understand why you were not informed.... I do not think, though, that you

should be too worried about the impact which MAUT made on the Board....

May I add a final word about the Academic Freedom and Tenure Committee? It is a body of volunteers, all of whom have more or less onerous duties at their own institutions, which meets five times annually. All its members have had experience of faculty association or union affairs, and of grievance matters. The Committee takes seriously its obligation to deal fairly and sensibly with the cases that arrive on the agenda. Conscious of the fact that any effectiveness it has depends upon the care with which the ground is prepared, the Committee will not intervene in a case—or advise the Board to intervene—unless it is sure of its position. The problem here is that we have not yet seen evidence or real argument that provides us with that necessary assurance. This is not to doubt your sincerity, nor is it to be biassed against you; but without a more solid basis than we now have at our disposal, I do not see that we can advise action. The very nature of your case may preclude such evidence from being produced. Your point that if we insist on solid evidence we may never act in cases of discrimination is well taken; but I do not see at present the answer to a real dilemma.

The CAUT board was not to be outdone. In a letter to Mandel, McGovern defended the board's behaviour:

You will, perhaps, not be surprised if I indicate that, in my judgement the Board handled a difficult issue as fairly as was possible in the circumstances.

First let me make clear that the Board has made no judgement either about the merits of your grievance or about the usefulness of the Gibson report in helping it to arrive at a decision on whether CAUT can or should do anything further to assist you. The Board decided, I think, reluctantly in view of the passage of time since the case arose, to defer a decision to its March 1983 meeting. It did so not only because the AF&T Committee suggested that it would appreciate an opportunity to comment fully on the report, but also, I think, because the Board members themselves had only received the report the previous day....

> In my view, the Board did not then and does not now perceive that the AF&T Committee is hostile to your case. Nor, I believe, does the Committee perceive itself in that way though clearly it has a view which differs from your own and from that of Professor Gibson on the strength of the case and on the procedures and responsibilities which should apply in making new appointments....
>
> I must disagree also with your view that the CAUT Board meeting was a "hearing." The Board meetings are open, though non-members, by custom, address the Board on invitation only. You and the representatives of MAUT sought and were given permission to address the Board. The MAUT, as a member organization of CAUT, had earlier expressed concern about the way in which the Board had become involved in the McGill cases and had requested an opportunity to address the Board on that issue.... I do feel, however, that when the MAUT presentation strayed into substantive issues in the cases under discussion it was stopped as promptly as was permitted by normal courtesy and the discretion allowed to visitors. My own judgement is that the MAUT intervention had little, if any, effect on the Board's consideration of the matter before it.
>
> I would like to point out finally that your allegations of political discrimination are an important aspect of your case, and the opinion of the Québec Human Rights Commission on this element is, I understand, judged by the AF&T Committee to be of significant value in assessing the findings of Professor Gibson.

The illogic and inconsistency of these explanations, which differed only in degree from the testimony of the various hostile witnesses in the two inquiries, did not augur well for Mandel's cause. The optimism generated by the CAUT report was fast dissolving. The McGill Department of Political Science was turning out to be more representative of the general attitudes in the Canadian academic community than Mandel had assumed.

The Second Blow

On March 26, 1983, CAUT once again considered the case. Mandel appeared before the board and for the second time appealed for action:

> The board now has before it the conclusions of the inquiry it itself established into my case concerning the unjust manner

in which I was deprived of an appointment at McGill University. These conclusions of the board's own committee have been supported by a second inquiry, that conducted under the auspices of the Québec Human Rights Commission according to the legal norms of evidence. No other evidence of even remotely comparable standing is before the board.

When I first brought my complaint to the CAUT in the spring of 1980, although I was confident that any neutral inquiry into the facts would justify my allegations, I nevertheless knew that there is always a risk that a complaint may be found to lack sufficient basis. I was prepared to accept this risk and to play by the rules that the board established. During these past three years I awaited the outcome of the CAUT's intervention. The outcome is now known. What I ask is that the board also play by these rules and it, accordingly, act on the recommendations of its own committee of inquiry and do so without procrastination or further delay.

Alluding to the AF&T document presumptuously entitled "Report to the Board on the Case of Dr. D. Mandel," he pointed out that there were no dissenting investigations: "Some other opinions have been brought to the board under the label of 'report' or 'comment'. They are all conjecture based upon partial and secondhand information."

Mandel concluded by noting first that

the evidence of improper motive in the form of these two reports is strong and clear, and this despite the fact, as the board's fact-finding committee observed, that the department "chose to adopt procedures which not only kept the reasons from the candidate, but also precluded their discovery by anyone else." Yet stronger proof could only be an admission by the decision-makers themselves of improper motive. To ask for such evidence is to wash one's hands of the entire issue of discrimination in academic hiring.

On the issue of Canadianization, he pointed to the following simple facts:

Had the CAUT's guidelines on "Canadianization" been observed, I would have been appointed....

> ...There is nothing in the CAUT's "Guidelines on Canadianization" to indicate that they are viewed by the CAUT any differently than its other guidelines on "Academic Appointment and Tenure." The preamble to the "Guidelines on Canadianization" states unequivocally:
>
>> The CAUT is always prepared to investigate any allegations of anti-Canadian discrimination and to endeavour to correct improper or unsatisfactory practices. If the Board should decide not to act on this flagrant violation of its own guidelines, then these guidelines should be removed from the CAUT Handbook, and, indeed, it would then be hard to see why the book should exist at all.

The board's response to Mandel was embodied in the following motion:

> Moved that since this Board believes that the evidence before it raises grave doubt about whether Dr. Mandel was treated fairly, McGill University be requested to join the CAUT to determine whether there was unfairness and to fix a remedy if appropriate and in anticipation of possible refusal by McGill of this proposal, a subcommittee of the CAUT Board be appointed by the Administration Committee to prepare a summary and analysis of the case for publication in the *CAUT Bulletin* and that in preparing the summary and analysis, the subcommittee consult with all interested parties and that the summary and analysis be presented to the June Board.

In a letter informing Mandel of the board's decision, McGovern acknowledged that the motion "will be a disappointment to you." Indeed, the motion recognized that doubts existed concerning McGill's treatment of Mandel. Instead of redress, however, it proposed... another inquiry. Then, anticipating McGill's refusal to cooperate, it "threatened" to publish a statement to be drafted by yet another committee!

In a letter that practically invited McGill's non-cooperation, McGovern wrote to Johnston:

> The CAUT Board has authorized me to invite McGill University to join with CAUT in conducting an investigation

of the case of Dr. David Mandel in order to determine whether there was unfairness in making the decision not to offer him an appointment. I am also authorized to suggest that the investigating body be provided with binding powers to fix a remedy, if appropriate.

...Serious questions about the fairness of the consideration of Dr. Mandel for appointment are raised in the report of the Gibson Committee. The report of the investigator for the Québec Human Rights Commission raises the same questions and provides additional detail on the events in question. While the CAUT Board is aware that the Commission itself decided to close the Mandel dossier it is the feeling of the Board that issues in the case which were not sufficiently persuasive to cause the Commission to intervene are nonetheless of concern to the Canadian academic community.

Based on their examination of the above document, it was apparent that members of the Board feel that there are matters arising from the case which led to the decision not to appoint Dr. Mandel and the allegation of discrimination which has been made....

The Board understands, of course, that the University has already declined proposals for binding adjudication on earlier occasions. It is the hope of the Board, however, that the University, in recognition of the importance of the issues raised by the Gibson Committee, will agree to the proposal on this occasion. It is my own view that the Canadian academic community will benefit from an objective examination of the problems which can arise in making appointments. The findings of an inquiry such as I am suggesting could lead to the development of guidelines which would make clear to applicants and universities the standards which will be maintained in making new appointments.

...I would, in any event, welcome an opportunity to discuss the case with you at your earliest convenience and to explain in greater detail why CAUT feels that the Mandel case will not have been satisfactorily resolved unless a way can be found to submit to final, binding examination, the issues which are of concern to the Canadian academic community.

The board met again in June. In what was now becoming routine procedure, Mandel, in a letter, expressed his disappointment and anger:

> It is deeply distressing to me that the subcommittee failed so woefully to carry out its mandate (a mandate that itself falls considerably short of what I feel is called for) and that the Board, on its part, does not appear even to have taken formal note of this. The Board's resolution of March 26 states that "in anticipation of possible refusal by McGill of this proposal, a subcommittee be appointed by the Administration Committee to prepare a summary and analysis of the case for publication in the *CAUT Bulletin* and that in preparing the summary and analysis the subcommittee consult with all interested parties and that the summary and analysis be presented to the June Board." The subcommittee did *not* prepare the summary and analysis for the June Board. The subcommittee did *not* consult with all interested parties, for it certainly did not consult with me. The subcommittee in fact reported on lines of argument to the June Board despite the instruction to present a *completed* report of which discussion with the parties was already a part—thus preempting the value of the discussion. The subcommittee in this matter so important to me ignored its mandate in all of these ways.
>
> After three years of waiting for the CAUT to bring this case to a positive conclusion, I am being told that I must be patient four months more (and how many more, perhaps, after that?), and no explanation is offered me—nor does any reasonable explanation of itself come to mind....
>
> Even more disturbing was the subcommittee's failure to consult with me before presenting the results of its work to the Board. In thus ignoring its mandate, the subcommittee has gravely prejudiced the outcome of the Board's deliberations and, frankly, it is hard for me to see how this subcommittee can now continue in good faith to carry out its task.
>
> As you know, the Board has before it two reports, one by its own fact-finding committee, which uphold my allegations of unjust treatment by McGill University. At the same time, the university has consistently, indeed, almost mockingly, rejected all proposals that it co-operate with the CAUT, to the point where Principal Johnston did not even

bother to respond to your letter on time for the June Board, as the resolution requested. At its March meeting, the Board decided on a course of action which included, among other things, the publication of a report on this case. This was not to be a new inquiry but part of the CAUT's efforts to redress the wrong done to me. I feel I have every reason to expect to be included as a full and direct participant in the drafting of this article. This, in fact, was the procedure followed by Dr. Hiller in two other McGill cases.

On June 11, Principal Johnston finally provided McGill's answer to the CAUT request for a further investigation:

You have asked McGill University to join with the CAUT in conducting a further investigation into the complaints of Dr. David Mandel. These complaints have already been investigated and considered several times over in various fora. These include complaints to the Québec Human Rights Commission and to a fact-finding committee appointed by you and chaired by Professor Gibson. In each case the complaints raised by Dr. Mandel have been discussed. The Gibson Committee Report made no finding on the specific complaints raised by Dr. Mandel, proceeded to identify a new issue not of Dr. Mandel's raising, and then came to certain conclusions on that new issue, which conclusions were rejected by a majority of the members of CAUT Academic Freedom and Tenure Committee.

In sum, Professor Mandel's complaints have been extensively analyzed at an enormous cost in time and expense. One could not justify yet another investigation into Professor Mandel's complaints. Thus, I regret to advise you that I cannot accede to your invitation.

CAUT by now had a new president, Professor Sarah J. Shorten. It fell to Shorten to explain to Mandel the position of CAUT in light of McGill's unwillingness to comply with its request:

The Board was, I believe, seriously concerned that the issue not be permitted to drag on longer than was unavoidable [*sic*]. They therefore wished, while providing every last opportunity for a resolution of the issue in cooperation with

McGill University, to set in place contingency arrangements to be implemented in the event that such a cooperative resolution proved unavailable. Publicizing the history of the case and the issues raised by it seemed to the Board our most appropriate strategy. In light of the contentions surrounding various reports previously produced, it was their view that a subcommittee not previously directly involved in controversy in this connection would be appropriate to produce this final report, to ensure maxima [*sic*] credibility and a "fresh eye" on the case. It remains clearly in the interests of all parties that the report be as accurate and as impartial as possible.

...The subcommittee selected consisted of Professor DeVlienger, of the University of Regina, and Professor Sagar, of Simon Fraser University, in addition to Professor Hiller, who was to act as resource person but explicitly not intended to play a leading or dominant role. In fact it proved necessary for him to provide a preliminary outline report which would serve as a starting document for modification, editing and finalization by the other members of the subcommittee. I must with regret report that while the preliminary document was available in June, the other members of the subcommittee had not had adequate opportunity to analyze and study it....

For these reasons, the Board adopted the following motion, subject to the understanding also minuted:

> THAT the Board authorize the subcommittee to proceed to finalize the draft report and to circulate it to interested parties and report to the Board in November.
>
> It was understood that the subcommittee wished to have Board input prior to its report in November and that the Board would receive a copy for comment, of the next draft of the report.

In a letter addressed to CAUT board members, Mandel made clear why he felt it no longer possible to participate in a procedure that had been corrupted:

> At its March meeting, the Board considered the report of its fact-finding committee (the Gibson report), which upheld my allegations of unfair treatment by McGill University....

In view of the fact that McGill has consistently rejected the CAUT's repeated requests for co-operation, the only logically consistent and fair way to proceed would have been to publish the report of the fact-finding committee as a first step toward rectifying the injustice.

But instead of this, the Board appointed a subcommittee "to prepare a summary and analysis of the case for publication in the *CAUT Bulletin* and (with the instruction) that in preparing the summary and analysis the subcommittee consult with all interested parties and that the summary and analysis be presented to the June Board." Five months have since elapsed. I have not received any statement explaining this decision or any account of the status of the report of the fact-finding committee. I have not received any information to show that the decision of the Board is being respected within the CAUT. In fact, no one has consulted with me. No summary and analysis were presented to the June Board....

Now I learn that this is not to be. Evidently the Board is not prepared to abide by its own decision. The President's letter as well as the June Board's resolution no longer refer to a "summary and analysis" but to a "report" and even a "final report." And so, the Board, for reasons which it has not seen fit to give me, is apparently dissatisfied with the report of its own fact-finding committee and is asking the subcommittee to produce a *new* report. In justification of this astonishing procedure, it is claimed that "in light of the contentions surrounding various reports previously produced, a subcommittee not previously involved in controversy in this connection would be appropriate to produce the final report, to ensure maxima [*sic*] credibility and a 'fresh eye' on the case. It remains clearly in the interests of all parties that the report be as accurate and as impartial as possible."

It is ludicrous to maintain that a subcommittee, whatever its composition, without having conducted any inquiry of its own, can produce a report that will improve on one that is the result of an independent investigation and whose conclusions are fully confirmed by yet a second independent inquiry. To seek accuracy and impartiality in such a fashion is on the face of it absurd.

There is also here a very disturbing intimation (heard not for the first time) that the members of the fact-finding committee are somehow less than impartial and tainted by controversy. Yet I am unaware of anything that would cast the slightest doubt on the credibility of this highly respected and eminently qualified panel. I find the implication outrageous. On the other hand, Dr. Hiller, one of the three members of the new subcommittee, author of its preliminary draft, chairs the Academic Freedom and Tenure Committee, which has issued an opinion recommending that the Board drop the case at once. And I am asked to believe that this procedure has been adopted in the interest of impartiality and accuracy!

But this is not the only way the Board has set aside its own resolution. Instead of the subcommittee consulting *me* in the process of drafting its summary and analysis and *before* it presents it to the Board, it is now the case that the subcommittee is consulting the *Board* in the process of drafting its "report," while I am to receive a draft of this "report" *at the same time* as the Board members, a draft that already incorporates the view of the Board members. Only *after* this, will any comments I have, be considered. The practical significance of the subcommittee's "consultation" with me is thus reduced to an empty formality....

...After three and a half years of placing my faith in a CAUT inquiry I am forced to question the genuineness of the CAUT's commitment to academic freedom, and particularly to the rights of the weakest members of the academic community, those still on the outside trying to build a career. It would appear that the primary concern of the CAUT, after all, is to avoid stepping on the toes of so large a faculty association as the MAUT and so powerful an institution as McGill University. And so, in the final analysis it all boils down to a question of power, so succinctly and cynically put by Joseph Stalin when asked about possible church reaction to his policy: "How many divisions has the Pope?"

Indeed, McGill and the MAUT have all the divisions. I have only the report of an independent inquiry by three academics that affirms that I was treated unjustly.

At this point, if the CAUT has any concern at all for equity and academic freedom, it must dissolve its subcommittee and publish the full report of its fact-finding committee.

The Third Blow

Mandel was now into his fourth year since the Political Science Department hiring decision. He had a half-time position as substitute professor at UQAM, which, along with his grant, gave him a reasonable income but no security for the future. His second book on the Russian Revolution was to appear that spring.

The board met again in early November 1983. It had before it yet another letter from Mandel insisting that it

> act in a manner consistent with your past actions and with the stated goals of the CAUT: to formally adopt the report of your fact-finding committee chaired by Professor Gibson, to request that McGill University carry out the recommendations of that report, and, in the event that McGill refuses, to begin procedures toward the censuring of McGill University on the double grounds of its unfair treatment of myself and its refusal to co-operate in a binding inquiry.

Confronted with the subcommittee's "Report to the Board on the Case of Dr. D. Mandel," he went on to comment that the "Report"

> is, finally, a ten-page-long non sequitur. On the one hand, its authors state that: "Although the CAUT Board felt that the investigations of the Mandel case were not conclusive, convergence of the available evidence gave grounds for disquiet [the March resolution said 'grave doubts'] at what occurred. It was impressed that the two independent investigations concluded that Dr. Mandel had probably [both reports stated this unequivocally] been treated unfairly. The Board felt that he was owed a final and conclusive inquiry. It is most regrettable that McGill University has been unwilling to clear the air in this way." And on the other hand... nothing! After my three-and-a-half years of seeking justice, after my vindication by two independent inquiries, the Board, according to the "Report to the Board on the Case of Dr. D. Mandel," decides that I am not deserving of any compensation... because McGill University, which is twice condemned by the inquiries, which has consistently refused to co-operate with the CAUT, has chosen to exercise a right to veto, so generously awarded it by the Board itself.

...By this inverted logic the CAUT ends up defending, not one of its members who has turned to it as a final recourse, but a university administration that has been found guilty by two inquiries and which has consistently refused to co-operate with the CAUT, an administration that has treated the CAUT with flagrant contempt.

Meanwhile, at the end of my three-and-a-half-year quest for justice, I learn to my amazement that the Board has never viewed me otherwise than as a guinea pig, a laboratory specimen. Yes, state the authors of the "Report to the Board on the Case of Dr. D. Mandel," there was indeed a blatant violation of the CAUT guidelines on "Canadianization." At some undefined point in the future the CAUT must decide if it will do anything about enforcing these guidelines—but certainly not in the Mandel case. Yes, they continue, the procedures adopted by the department left the door wide open to the play of illegitimate considerations and these procedures did indeed result in an unfair decision. The CAUT will have to decide at some unspecified time in the future how to deal with this—but not in the Mandel case. McGill University, which already stands twice condemned by the only two inquiries, has refused to co-operate in a third binding inquiry. Here the "Report to the Board on the Case of Dr. D. Mandel" does not even suggest that there is a problem the CAUT must deal with, even though the de facto veto its authors would give to McGill renders any recourse to the CAUT absolutely meaningless.

It is unconscionable that representatives of the Canadian academic community should adopt such an unjust and illogical position, one whose message to university administrations is that the CAUT will do nothing to prevent the rule of arbitrariness and injustice in the treatment of candidates applying for posts. The message to the candidates is no less clear: if you are thinking of complaining to the CAUT, know that you will end up worse off than you began.

Mandel's views on the draft "report" and the interventions by the AF&T committee were echoed by members of the CAUT fact-finding committee in separate communications to Dr. Sim.

Keith Johnstone objected to the "report's" suggestion that the Gibson committee should have provided information on matters which it was not empowered to investigate: "It was not forgetfulness which prevented the fact-finding committee from reporting, for example, on the voting pattern in the Department of Political Science or on the views of individual members of the department." Johnstone reminded the board that he and his colleagues did not have subpoena powers and had no access to the individual voting record in the department on the Mandel appointment. The criticism implied in the observation of the AF&T majority "report" that the fact-finding committee "tells nothing about the other candidates that supports its conclusions" ignores the fact that it was not possible for the fact-finding committee to compare the candidates in the manner suggested. It could only determine whether, in its view, Mandel was fairly treated. "It was possible for McGill University to provide information on other candidates which would have allayed concern about Dr. Mandel's treatment.... The onus was on the University to do so. It did not take the opportunity." Johnstone concluded that the publication of the AF&T Committee's commentary on the case in the *CAUT Bulletin* would not bring credit to CAUT.

Côté, for his part, stated that the section "Responses of the Board" is "unbelievable."

> The fact-finding committee was established because McGill University had declined an invitation to establish a joint committee of inquiry.... It was ridiculous to again ask the University to agree to a hearing on the case.... The Board should be censuring the University and not the fact-finding committee.... If the only result of the Board decision to establish a fact-finding committee is to be the proposed account in the *Bulletin* why did the Board establish the Gibson committee in the first place?... To allow McGill University to opt out of the CAUT guidelines on Canadianization, as the draft report does, places the status of all CAUT guidelines in jeopardy.... The fact-finding committee took as part of its mandate the task of determining whether the guidelines had been followed. It decided that they had not.

Finally, Gibson, chair of the fact-finding committee, stated that he was "resentful" about the way in which the careful report of the fact-finding committee had been considered by the AF&T

committee and the board. The three demanded that the complete report of the fact-finding committee be published.

Faced with this revolt by its own committee, at its November meeting the board resolved:

> THAT the Board authorize publication in the *CAUT Bulletin* as soon as possible, of
>
> a) an article which states the findings of the Gibson report as it pertains to the case of Dr. Mandel;
>
> b) a statement by the President of CAUT expressing the findings of this Board; and
>
> c) an article expressing the concerns relating to procedures for initial appointments as suggested by the Gibson report.

This motion was clarified in a letter to CAUT President Shorten from Gibson:

> I am writing, as I said I would, to record my understanding of the conclusions reached at the meeting with Ken McGovern and yourself this morning....
>
> I understand that the CAUT Board has agreed to the publication of the Fact-Finding Committee's report in the *CAUT Bulletin* with such editorial changes as the Committee will agree to. While my colleagues and I are unwilling to make substantial changes in the content or style of the report, I have undertaken to give the material a final polish, as well as to remove, for publication purposes, the documentary appendix....
>
> Ken McGovern suggested that the two parts of our report be published as separate units, though in the same issue, and that they be accompanied by a third unit, which would be your commentary on behalf of the Board. I agree.

Mandel had requested that Gibson and his colleagues take a stronger public stand on the board's treatment of their report. But this was not forthcoming. Gibson conveyed his position in a letter to Jack Weldon:

> I personally think that the Fact-Finding Committee is more likely to be influential in this matter if we stand on our

Report rather than becoming involved in the details of its implementation. There were suspicions in some quarters at McGill about partisanship by the Committee, and I think that anything the Committee does which can be distorted to took like corroboration of those suspicions will be harmful in the long run.

Yet once again the board failed to implement its own resolution. And once again Mandel sent off his ritual letter of complaint to Shorten:

> I received today from Dr. Sim a package containing a revised version of the Gibson Report as well as the "Report of the A.F. and T. Committee on the Mandel Case and on the Fact-Finding Committee Report." In a telephone conversation today, Dr. Sim explained that the latter was being published in fulfillment of the board's resolution. However, he called back a few minutes later to correct this, saying that, in fact, the A.F. and T. Committee had requested its publication, and the board was acceding in accord with the *Bulletin*'s editorial policy of allowing the expression of the broadest possible opinion, especially on so "controversial" a case as my own....
>
> Regardless of where the request came from... the A.F. and T. Committee is a committee of the board, and if its "report" is being published it is because the board has decided to do so. This violates the November resolution of the board as well as the agreement between yourself and Dr. Gibson as set out in his November 22 letter to you. In neither case is there any mention of publication of the A.F. and T. Committee's "report."
>
> Moreover, in your December 7 letter to Dr. Gibson you wrote that the CAUT would *not* be soliciting comments from interested parties.... Yet the package that is being sent out by Dr. Sim is nothing if not solicitation by the CAUT.
>
> I wish to protest in the strongest possible terms this violation—the latest in a whole series—by the board, of its own word.

In the next few days I will be sending off to the *Bulletin*'s editor the following three items for publication:

1. a letter summing up my view of the board's handling of my case
2. my statement to the March 1983 board, which is a response to the A.F. and T. Committee's "report"
3. my summary of the report of the investigator for the Québec Human Rights Commission.

Dr. Sim expressed some concern about the length of the latter. However, it is shorter than the A.F. and T. Committee's "report." As the only other competent report by a neutral party (the other is, of course, the Gibson report), its publication is certainly in accord with the *Bulletin*'s policy of allowing the broadest possible expression of opinion. By contrast, the A.F. and T. Committee's "report" is based upon no inquiry and it was not written by a neutral body—the A.F. and T. Committee opposed the unilateral establishment of an inquiry (you can check with Dr. Jill Vickers, who was head of the A.F. and T. Committee at the time).

Not With a Bang, But With a Whimper

The case was coming to a close, but not before one more effort by Mandel to at least obtain an explanation of the board's actions. In December he had sent a letter to CAUT President Shorten:

> Dr. Sim has informed me by telephone of the decision of the November board concerning my case. He also promised me that I would soon receive from you a written report of this decision, including an explanation of the reasoning behind it.
>
> ...At the end of my three-and-a-half years of dealing with the CAUT on this matter, I feel that I—as well as the entire Canadian academic community—are owed an honest and coherent explanation for the board's decision. In particular, I would like *direct* and *specific* answers to the following questions:
>
> 1. In light of the fact-finding committee's conclusion that the Department of Political Science "chose to adopt procedures that not only kept the reasons [for not hiring

me] from the candidate, but also precluded their discovery by anyone else," what *concrete* evidence would the board have considered sufficient to allow it to act against McGill University in this case?

2. By what authority and on the basis of what criteria does the board decide that some of the CAUT's guidelines are meant to be taken seriously and to be enforced while others are not? Specifically, why do the "Guidelines on Canadianization" appear in successive editions of the *Handbook* if the board now claims that the CAUT did not intend that they be acted upon?

3. The board has stated that it has "grave doubts" about whether I was treated fairly by McGill University. These doubts moved it to call for a new joint inquiry. McGill's refusal blocked this inquiry. As a result, the board has decided that it can proceed no further with my complaint. This means that in practice the CAUT makes its action in defence of academic freedom dependent upon the co-operation of the university administration that is responsible for the violation of academic freedom. Is this a general policy of the CAUT? If not, on what basis does the CAUT decide where such a policy should apply?

Shorten answered in February 1984:

Subsequently, as I have reported to you, the Board decided, following extensive debate after your presentation before it in November, to publish the full findings of the Gibson Committee. This is a course of action that I interpret your previous representations to advocate. The Board, in making this decision, was, I believe, reiterating the serious concerns expressed in the March resolution.

The action of publication of this very full account is by no means an insignificant one by the CAUT. It is indeed a statement of genuine and serious concern to the academic community of Canada.

I therefore disagree with the premises on which the first three questions of your letter of November 21st are based. Your first question suggests that the Board has decided not to act against McGill University. Publication of the case in the *Bulletin*, in the form of the report of the Gibson Committee, is such an act, in my view, which I believe to be that of the Board also.

Your second question implies that the Board has decided that some of CAUT's guidelines are not to be taken seriously. Certainly, the Board has taken no such decision. However, I would point out to you that CAUT guidelines, while intended to influence and inform procedure in Canada's universities, do not constitute legal constraint on either faculty associations or university administrations. Some guidelines such as those regarding academic appointments and tenure have a directness and specificity which permits a more direct and specific application. Others such as those on Canadianization enunciate general principles which are indeed seriously meant but which foresee an exhortatory use. They do not provide arguments based on natural justice for application in particular cases. Where they are violated, the CAUT publicly expresses its concern. I am interested in your view that the Board claims that CAUT did not intend its guidelines to be acted upon. Perhaps you have been misinformed.

Your third question states that the Board has decided that it can proceed no further with your complaint, as a result of McGill University's refusal to co-operate in an inquiry. The publication of the Gibson Report is one form such action can take: this is the course of action now being pursued by the Board. You appear to suggest that perhaps the CAUT should further pursue an inquiry with McGill. The university has repeatedly and unequivocally refused. We have no means of coercion.

I regret your continued vilification of the CAUT Board in connection with your case. I believe the members of the Board have pursued continuously the goal of securing a full inquiry into what happened. Its members have repeatedly stated and acted upon the concern that they feel. I believe you misjudge them.

Mandel responded to her letter:

I have received your letter of February 3 in response to my request for an explanation of the board's decision on my case. Unfortunately, you seem to have misunderstood the import of my questions. To this day I have not been told what the status of the Gibson report is in the eyes of the board. Judging from the board's November resolution, I conclude that it has not adopted the report. I am asking a very simple and direct question: why? I expect an equally simple and direct reply. I have not yet received this.

Your letter indicates that the board does not consider the Gibson inquiry to have been a full one. ("I believe that the members of the board have pursued continuously the goal of securing a full inquiry into what happened.") This is the first time I have heard such an opinion. Why do you not consider the Gibson inquiry a full inquiry? (You will recall that its conclusions are fully supported by the only other inquiry conducted, one which heard over fifty hours of testimony.) What sort of new evidence would the board be seeking from such a "full inquiry"? I put this question to you in my letter of November 23 but I have received no reply.

I am well aware that the CAUT has no means to force a university to participate in a joint inquiry. My point was rather that if a joint inquiry is made a condition of any effective CAUT action (and in my case this would be formal adoption by the board of the report of its own fact-finding committee and its conclusions and eventually, if necessary, censure), the board is in effect allowing the accused party, the university administration, to block with impunity the pursuit of justice. I asked you in my letter if this was CAUT policy in all cases where administrations refuse to co-operate in inquiries, and again, you did not answer.

You draw the crucial distinction between CAUT guidelines that permit direct and specific application and those meant for exhortatory use. This is the first I have heard of such a distinction. Certainly the members of the CAUT are unaware of it, and there would appear to be no lawful basis for it within the CAUT. I do not understand why the Canadianization Guidelines do not allow direct and specific application. I was the sole Canadian among the two dozen candidates. The department, while agreeing that I was qualified, was unable to justify its preference for a non-Canadian. Had the guidelines been respected, the job would have been mine. This is very direct and specific.

You further state that where the guidelines are violated, the CAUT publicly expresses its concern. This has not been done in my case. The publication of the Gibson report cannot be considered an expression of concern, since it was not adopted by the board.

You write that the board has indeed acted upon my case. The board's grudging and belated agreement to publish the full report of its own committee (a year and a half after its appearance and only upon the insistence of its authors), alongside the assessment of people who have never investigated and who are hostile to that report, and in circumstances that suggest that the board has no intention of going further can perhaps be termed action, but is of no use to me. I have wasted my time pursuing this grievance through the CAUT over the course of the past three-and-a-half years and for all my trouble I have not even received a logically coherent explanation for the board's so-called "action."

Finally, I must take exception to your use of the term "vilification" to describe my protest against the board's handling of the Gibson report. After being unjustly deprived of a post that was mine according to the only two inquiries conducted, after vainly seeking redress through the CAUT for three-and-a-half years, I have every right to express in the frankest possible terms my view of the board's conduct: it has been beneath all criticism. For you to turn legitimate protest into "vilification" is unjust and does discredit to the organization that you head.

Postscript

The Gibson Report was published in the April 1984 issue of the *CAUT Bulletin*, exactly four years after the McGill Political Science Department had rejected its Appointments Committee's recommendation that Mandel be given the tenure-track post in Soviet and East European politics.

As Mandel had expected, there was no indication in the *Bulletin* of CAUT's attitude to the report. But the appearance alongside it of the AF&T committee's report, and comments from MAUT and the McGill administration, left no doubt that CAUT had turned its back on the Gibson committee.

The *Bulletin* did, however, publish a letter from Mandel, in which he further "vilified" CAUT and concluded by asking

Canadian academics if they cared enough about academic freedom "to do something about this organization that purports to speak in their name." This final *cri de coeur* elicited virtually no response. Apparently those who did care had concluded that CAUT was not worth their trouble. This was the reasoning of the members of the Gibson committee: they had already wasted enough time.

One person who did react was Jill Vickers, former chair of the AF&T committee, who wrote Mandel:

> I see from the latest *CAUT Bulletin* that my forebodings about your case were accurate. You will recall that the AF&T Committee was originally opposed to CAUT taking up your case (and the others at McGill).... I am increasingly persuaded that the issue of fair hiring will be the "rock" on which CAUT will eventually founder—unless it is prepared to see AF&T style "collegiality" for what it is.

The April *Bulletin* was the sum total of CAUT's "action" on Mandel's behalf. Sim had assured him that the board would soon be taking up the report's general recommendations on hiring guidelines. As of December 1986 there are still no guidelines.

McGill, meanwhile, launched its "campaign for excellence" in an effort to increase its private funding. Principal Johnston has also been active with the administrative heads of the other Québec and Canadian universities in opposing state cuts to higher education. Yet the university continues to hire non-Canadians, whenever it sees fit, and continues to go unchallenged. The senior members of the Political Science Department, whose testimony both the Gibson Committee and the Human Rights investigation found incredible, have put the "unpleasantness" behind them and gone on in their selfless pursuit of knowledge. The junior members who voted against Mandel without being able to coherently explain their action, or who failed to support Mandel in his appeal, have since obtained tenure.

Mandel is still in Montréal and is still a substitute professor half-time, teaching courses that are at times far from his area of specialization. He has continued with his research on the Soviet Union and has compiled a respectable publications record.

He is also still a Marxist and continues to be active on the radical left.

In the intervening years, a few tenure-track jobs in his field have been advertised, and despite his reluctance to leave Montréal Mandel applied for these. In two cases he was invited to interviews—for positions at Queen's and Memorial Universities. In the former case, a professor later wrote him that "it is your misfortune, and ours, that the final decision concerning this appointment was made without adequate consideration being given to scholarship." Regarding Mandel's other applications, he merely received form letters thanking him for applying and telling him what a good field of candidates it was this year (chocolate, vanilla, raspberry, as Barbara Haskel had so graphically put it). There is no real basis to suspect blacklisting or political bias, of course. But that is just the point—with no obligation on the part of the university to explain appointment decisions and no possibility of appeal, can there ever be a basis?

Mandel refused the invitation to an interview for a post at Memorial because he had learned that the university was under CAUT censure. James Hiller, chair of the AF&T committee and a history professor at Memorial, wrote a letter to Mandel which—coming as it did at the end of the case—epitomized the seriousness of CAUT's commitment to academic freedom:

> Let me reiterate that CAUT cannot reasonably expect junior or unemployed academics to refuse offers from universities that are under censure. This is well understood within the Association, and accepted as necessary given the existing job market. It does nothing to strengthen the credibility of censure, but people have careers to look after. I understand the dilemma in which you find yourself, and do not presume to offer advice. I can only say that I do not think anyone would blame you if you were to accept a position at a censured institution.

There was one other, rather curious, piece of correspondence from Hiller to Mandel, a handwritten note dated February 19, 1983: "I have just received a copy of your letter to the *CAUT Bulletin* dated 18/2. On page 3 you refer to Memorial University as 'a small institution.' [Referring to CAUT's cowardice, Mandel had written: "It is not too risky to censure a small institution like Memorial University especially when the local faculty association is supporting the victim. But to take on so powerful and prestigious a university as McGill is another matter, all the more so as the executive of the local faculty association, the MAUT, well known for its intimate ("collegial") relations with the administration, has from the start opposed CAUT interventions."] This is a factual inaccuracy. I do not have exact student and faculty figures at hand, but they are in the order of 8,170 and 700 respectively."

Conclusion: Academic Freedom and Accountability

The CAUT board never officially pronounced itself on the report of its fact-finding committee. In practice, of course, there is no doubt that it rejected the report. Its inaction—and publication of the report—without comment, alongside the AF&T committee's rebuttal, speak for themselves. Try as he did (and toward the end the letters were flying fast and furious), Mandel was unable to move the board to formulate, let alone justify, its position on the report.

In the course of pursuing his grievance, Mandel met repeatedly with the refusal to explain a position on academic hiring that on the very face of it was untenable. At an early point in his dealings with CAUT, he was informed by its executive secretary, Victor Sim, that even the strongest evidence might not induce CAUT to act. Three years later, Sarah Shorten, CAUT president, simply ignored Mandel's repeated questions as to what evidence the board would consider sufficient to warrant action.

It was never a question of evidence or the strength of the case. More than three years after the Gibson committee presented its carefully argued proposals, CAUT still has no guidelines on academic hiring. Clearly, there is reluctance in the profession to deal with the issue. The president of the Canadian Political Science Association, F.C. Engelmann, in a letter dated June 17, 1985, relating the decision of his board not to urge McGill to submit the Mandel case to binding arbitration, wrote that "departments are not responsible to the profession for initial appointments to a tenure-track position and... the association should not attempt to persuade a university to enforce such a responsibility." However, he went on to observe, the board "may well have decided differently if Professor Mandel had been victimized, really or apparently, for his persuasion while holding a tenure-track or tenured position." Again, no explanation for this apparently incongruous position.

One of the Gibson committee's proposals was that criteria for new posts be clearly specified in advance. This point was also made by the investigator for the Québec Human Rights Commission (HRC) in a question to Dean Vogel:

> [In the Vaillancourt case, the inquiry found] that the preliminary criteria were not set to start out with or that certain criteria were invoked after the fact, certain requirements for the post were not known before. And now one sees in the inquiry into the Mandel case that the department functioned in hiring Mme Debardeleben without having fixed criteria for the post as such.... How can one reproach a candidate for not meeting criteria if these criteria were not established from the start?

The only answer Vogel could offer was: "Your idea of putting up a list of criteria and matching candidates... may be a fine thing. But I mean, no one does it."

Thus, no one seemed able or willing to explain a position, the practical import of which is to leave departments free to hire by any arbitrary or tainted criteria and procedures they may choose.

It is puzzling that a profession that claims to take academic freedom so seriously should be willing to deny any guarantees of this academic freedom in hiring; it thus not only gives departments the freedom to deny entry to people who are professionally and politically outside the mainstream, but also allows free use of blacklisting. It is not necessary to conjure up another Joe McCarthy in order to appreciate the abuses such a stand makes possible. If universities are careful enough in their initial hiring, there will be little need to fire people later for non-academic reasons. "Deviants" who make it through the graduate school selection process are left unprotected as they seek employment.

The silence of these representatives of the profession when it comes to their refusal to deal meaningfully with Mandel's grievance and their rejection of guidelines on hiring makes one wonder if this is not an embarrassed silence. After all, these are trained academics whose job it is to explain. Could it be that they are unable to come up with a legitimate explanation?

The Gibson report noted that "CAUT has concerned itself in the main with the welfare of those who already have at least one foot inside a university portal, to the exclusion of those who are merely knocking at the door." Actually, even before Mandel, CAUT had looked into the issue of hiring and in 1980 adopted a document. But, commented the Gibson committee, "that document seems more concerned with the collective rights of existing faculty members to participate in the appointments process, than with the individual rights of the applicants or appointments." The Gibson report explained this by offering that "altruism is the final and most fragile layer of the civil veneer. Canadian university professors and their national association have had their hands full devising satisfactory procedural safeguards in matters that concern them personally and directly."

We would take this argument a major step further. This absence of altruism is not simply due to a shortage of time and energy: there is a perceived and real conflict of interests involved. The sorry fact is that most academics—or most of those who control hiring, at least—do not want guarantees that would limit their "freedom" (or licence) to hire who they want, even if this involves the application of non-academic and tainted criteria. Anyone familiar with the university appointments process will know that this "freedom" is exercised by no means infrequently.

The decision not to appoint Mandel was not really extraordinary, then. What *was* different here is his stubborn insistence that the decision be justified. His demand, if unprecedented, was certainly not unreasonable—especially given the fact that since Mandel was the nominee of the Appointments Committee the department had to reject him before considering other candidates. The immigration law (at least its spirit), as well as CAUT guidelines on "Canadianization," also required that the department find Mandel—the only Canadian of some dozen candidates—unqualified, before it went on to consider others. In other words, his rejection had to involve more than a "global judgement" or the choice of "one among many qualified candidates." There had to be specific reasons why the department, for the first time in a decade, turned aside the proposal of its Appointments Committee.

Mandel's demands for an explanation might seem perfectly reasonable. But at McGill—and apparently in the larger academic community as well, judging by CAUT's silence on the Gibson report proposals—this violated a sacred norm. As MAUT President Handa put it, "that it would seriously contaminate this area of university life [appointments] if such a procedure were adopted [providing rejected candidates with reasons] is part of the common wisdom of the profession. [It would cause] great damage... to the university."

The Gibson report took up the major arguments against guidelines on hiring and convincingly showed that the concern about "great damage" was really unfounded. In fact, it suggested a workable set of guidelines for fair appointment practices (see Appendix I). The "great damage" would be done, in reality, not to the university, but rather to the "freedom" of academics to choose new colleagues whether or not the basis for their choice is legitimate.

Nayar's testimony comparing the selection of a person for an academic post to a political election is revealing of how academics really view the hiring process. Politics are about interests, and people will vote for the candidate who they think will best further their interests. In this context, the requirement to explain or justify a vote obviously makes no sense. In comparing a political election to university hiring, Nayar implied that academics choose new colleagues according to their personal interests. Official academic values, however, dictate that appointments be made on the basis of objective academic standards. Such appointments, unlike political voting, can and should be justified if challenged.

What Nayar was in effect saying, and what the Mandel case shows, is that most Canadian academics are unwilling to make hiring decisions subject to the same guarantees that tenure and promotion decisions enjoy. Theirs is a "proprietary" attitude toward their department. These "property rights" include the right to choose colleagues who will be "collegial."

Attempts to limit this "right" are met with the same outrage and stubborn resistance shown by factory owners and their management when faced with union demands or government regulations that would limit their right to freely dispose of their capital. This is also why the CAUT guidelines on Canadianization have never been enforced.

The guarantees that *do* exist in promotion and tenure decisions *do* limit academics' "right to fire." But these guarantees are there to protect their own corporatist interests. It might be nice, of course, to be able to get rid of a competent colleague who, for one reason or another, is not to one's personal liking—and such attempts do occur, as we saw in the Noumoff and Vaillancourt cases. But the general corporate interests of academics would obviously not be served by the introduction of arbitrariness into their own midst. Just the opposite: it would threaten their own job security.

But university professors *do not own* their departments. If they are permitted to run them more or less autonomously, it is not so that they can freely pursue their own interests, but because such autonomy is considered the best means to further the pursuit of knowledge—which, after all, is the *raison d'être* of the university.

Mandel's grievance did more than simply challenge the *de facto* rights of academics, however. He claimed to be the victim of the application of not merely arbitrary criteria, but of criteria that were political. This was another major breach of academic norms. The university, an institution that bases its very existence upon the principle of free inquiry, was accused of harbouring people who would reject a candidate because they did not like his politics. The university's response was revealingly aggressive: it accused the inquiries of violating academic freedom by investigating professors' political beliefs.

At its meeting of May 12, 1982, the McGill Senate, the university's senior administrative body, for the first and only time took recognition of Mandel's grievance. It considered a motion stating:

> In the inherently coercive atmosphere of an official hearing, some of our colleagues were asked to reveal their own religious and political beliefs and to make judgments about the beliefs of others. Such questions, pursuant to beliefs rather than acts, are an offense to civil liberty and a threat to academic freedom. Questions of this nature should never be permitted in Human Rights proceedings.

Over the course of fifty hours, twenty-one witnesses provided testimony before the Human Rights Commission. Yet the Senate, after a brief and perfunctory discussion, during which the phrase "inherently coercive atmosphere of" was deleted, passed the resolution without dissent. The vast majority of its members had only the vaguest idea of the issues involved in Mandel's grievance. Apparently only two senators (of the fifty-one present) had bothered to look at the hearing transcripts. The seconder of the motion later admitted that he had acted on the basis of inadequate information but that he had taken the motion to be a statement of "abstract principle."

The principle was, of course, that one should not besmirch the university by casting doubt on its selfless devotion to the pursuit of knowledge; thus opening the way to outside intervention into university affairs. The Senate motion was, of course, a tactic promoted by members of the Political Science Department in an effort to ensure themselves university support in the event of a condemnatory report by the HRC. But this issue of tactics was probably secondary for most of those involved, who saw themselves as defending "academic freedom" in the face of outside scrutiny of university behaviour. It will be recalled that even CAUT's intervention in the form of a fact-finding committee, itself an academic body, had been given a hostile reception at McGill and had been described by MAUT as a form of tyranny.

The prevailing view in academia is that the preservation of academic freedom requires the university to protect itself from outside pressures, and, in particular, from those that might be exerted by the state. This view would have merit if it resulted in the university actually taking an aggressive stand in defence of the principle of free inquiry. This has not been the case, however, at least in North America, where universities have generally been able to establish a special tacit relationship with the state and those interests in society who benefit from the existing socio-economic structure that the state protects. In practice, this has meant that in return for its relative autonomy, the university is expected to police its own members.

This has generally not been a terribly onerous obligation. Academics, perhaps even more than other people, find it comfortable in the mainstream. They are not, on the whole, a very courageous lot, and even if they do enjoy certain guarantees in terms of job tenure, the life of nonconformists, especially those who are active on the left, can be made very unpleasant and difficult.

But the most effective, and, therefore, preferred policing mechanism is that which is brought into play even before the "trouble-maker" can become part of the university. It is a wonderfully simple mechanism: merely declare that the candidate has no rights. As Engelmann, the president of the Canadian Political Science Association, stated in his letter: "It is clear that arbitration involves *rights*, and that no one has the right to be appointed to a tenure-track position." With no rights, the candidate cannot even learn the basis for the decision, and so there can be no grievance. Thus, policing can occur without anyone outside the department knowing about it, and the ideology of academic freedom remains intact. In this context we cannot but agree with MAUT President Handa that to act to rectify the injustice in the Mandel case or to adopt the proposed guidelines on hiring would cause "great damage to the university." But the "university" to which Handa refers bears no relation to the university concerned with the pursuit and dissemination of knowledge.

The university has been able to get away with the claim that candidates have no rights largely because that claim fits in well with the dominant practice in our society that guarantees employers, as property owners, the right to hire and fire. We have already seen why academics' corporate interests have led them to enact some guarantees against arbitrary firing. But hiring is another matter. In asserting that candidates have no right to jobs, Engelmann was merely applying a general principle of our society—no one has the right to any particular job, or for that matter, to any job at all. Therefore, if a job applicant claims that he or she has been the victim of illegal discrimination in hiring, the burden of proof falls on the candidate, not the owner. But Engelmann forgot that the university is not a business enterprise, whose goal is to achieve the greatest return on capital. Universities are supposed to be special institutions devoted to the pursuit of knowledge. If this is a real goal, then the most qualified candidate for a post does indeed have a right to that post, and it is logically incumbent on the university to show that the rejected candidate was not the most qualified of the applicants, all the more so since the candidate almost never has access to the information that would allow him or her to prove the complaint.

This is the conclusion at which the Gibson committee arrived. Unfortunately, the HRC, as an institution of the capitalist state, does not work according to that principle. The commission always places the burden of proof on the employee or the aspiring employee. It is therefore not surprising that the commission has never won a university hiring complaint. Unlike business enterprises, universities can make arguments that claim to be based on highly specialized knowledge that the commissioners will rarely feel competent to assess. This is also the reason why the immigration authorities generally refuse to intervene in academic hiring to enforce the immigration law.

Although our main concern here is with the academic world, a few words on the HRC are in order. Our experience with the commission leads us to conclude that, like the idea of "academic freedom," it plays an essentially ideological role. It is there to create the impression that there really is recourse against the wealthy and powerful. The woefully inadequate funding and staffing of the HRC attests to the fact that our state does not take the commission's avowed role seriously.

Mandel's case from begining to end took twenty-six months—and that was expeditious treatment. Moreover, during those twenty-six months, he had to devote a considerable amount of his time to the inquiry. He was told at the outset that McGill's lawyer would be present and that he would do well to bring one of his own. For a few months, the Federation of University Professors of Québec (FAPUQ) supplied counsel free of charge, but then inexplicably withdrew it. Mandel was fortunate to have Allen Fenichel, a McGill economist, as adviser throughout the entire hearing. There were, however, several times when the absence of legal counsel was keenly felt. In any case, how many ordinary "working stiffs" could find the necessary resources... and the patience?

The inquiry report, which was well over a hundred pages long, was disposed of by the HRC in a matter of minutes. Only after much effort was Mandel able to obtain an explanation of this decision. It took the form of a one-and-a-quarter-page document, which did not even hint that the Commission had received a favourable report. Only after several more months of pressure did he obtain a copy of that report and learn that the inquiry had upheld his allegations.

The Human Rights Commission has since repeated itself. In another complaint of discrimination in hiring at Université de Montréal, a report of more than a thousand pages (the case took five years), submitted in 1986, upheld the allegations, but the Commission overturned the decision. Months have gone by, and the plaintiff, Robert Cadotte, is still trying to get an explanation.

We would not want our analysis, however, to lead to fatalistic resignation among those who have a genuine commitment to academic freedom. Our universities, like all institutions, are inevitably subject to constraints imposed by the society in which they operate. But we are not functionalists who believe that all institutions inevitably work to maintain the social system in which they exist. How they function at any time will depend upon the particular correlation of forces in that institution and in the larger society.

Academic freedom is an ideology in our society and is destined to remain one.[1] But for an ideology to be at all efficient, it must have some basis in reality, and this means that "deviants" can and do make it through the graduate school and hiring processes, especially when the political climate is benign and academic jobs are plentiful. Moreover, once inside, they can defend themselves (if their performance has been well above average) by using the general rules that academics have enacted to protect themselves against arbitrary dismissal. These "deviants," despite the efforts made to get rid of them, are then used to show that academic freedom, despite occasional lapses, is "on the whole" alive and well.

Those committed to the pursuit of knowledge—and particularly the kind of knowledge that can help build a more democratic and just society—have an obligation to work towards broadening the limits to genuine academic freedom, even if this involves the risk of disapproval by colleagues and damage to one's career.

It is this commitment that made us pursue this grievance to the bitter end, even though fairly early on it became clear that the immediate cause—justice for Mandel—was a lost one. It is also this commitment that made us decide to write this book. It is our hope that it will ultimately make some contribution, however modest, to enlarging the space in our universities for those who believe that pursuit of knowledge should be more than the search for technocratic means to more efficiently manage the status quo.

The other major issue raised by Mandel's case, "Canadianization," might seem at first glance to contradict our concern for

---

[1] For an interesting elaboration of this thesis, see B. Ollman, "Academic Freedom in America Today, a Marxist View," *Monthly Review*, Vol. 35, No. 10, March 1984.

academic freedom. It introduces into hiring the criterion of citizenship, a criterion that, on the face of it, has nothing to do with the pursuit and dissemination of knowledge. The argument that "we have to be free to choose the best person" is a favourite of those opposed to "Canadianization," including MAUT, which has explicitly rejected CAUT's avowed policy.

On November 19, 1980, MAUT put a resolution before the McGill Senate. Its preamble stated:

> When candidates are considered for new academic posts, the determining factors in the hiring decisions should be the academic qualifications of the candidate without consideration of "accidental" factors such as place of birth or previous place of legal residence.

After passage of the motion concerning advertising practices, Vice-Principal Yaffe moved that the Senate endorse the preamble itself. In the ensuing debate, it was pointed out that the Senate had already agreed to the preamble when it passed the motion. Principal Johnston argued that passing the preamble separately might cause problems with CAUT, the House of Commons, and immigration officials. But Yaffe was not satisfied. The university should not be intimidated by immigration bureaucrats, he stated. Although the motion was tabled, McGill had clearly put on record its intention of violating the law. Since then, it has continued to hire non-Canadians, and we are not aware of any case in which immigration officials have refused to issue the necessary papers.

The arguments advanced against "Canadianization," "academic freedom," and the "unfettered pursuit of excellence" are often smoke screens put forth by those opposed to any restriction on the hiring powers of university staff and administrations. We have already seen the negligible role that "academic excellence" really played in the Mandel case.

To begin with, the "Canadianization" criteria does not call for the exclusive hiring of Canadians. It requires that competent Canadians, where available, be given priority, and that a university wishing to appoint a non-Canadian be prepared to justify that choice. It could conceivably be the case that no qualified Canadian is available to fill a senior post requiring a particularly high level of proven competence in a specialized field. But this could hardly be true of a junior appointment where judgement of competence is based on potential rather than on actual achievement.

Moreover, the pursuit of knowledge does not take place in a social vacuum. The very questions a teacher or researcher asks, and the methodology used, are determined by his or her social background and world view, as well as by more immediate social and political interests and concerns. We pay for our universities through our taxes, and we have a legitimate right to expect that they take up issues of concern to us as Canadians. A study of Canadian content in political science courses found a clear relationship between the proportion of Canadian staff in a department and the amount of attention paid to Canadian subject matter.[2] In 1975, the *Report of the Commission on Canadian Studies* of the Association of Universities and Colleges of Canada noted that

> In a large number of political science departments in Canada... American priorities and methodologies have substantially shaped the character, not only of research programmes, but of undergraduate and graduate course offerings as well. In part, at least, this development must be related to the large number of political scientists in Canada who are not Canadians.[3]

According to Statistics Canada, in 1973-74, 35.6% of political science staff were non-Canadians, including 22% who were U.S. citizens.[4] In 1980-81, in the social sciences generally, 28.2% were non-Canadians (18.3% U.S. citizens).[5] For new, full-time appointments in which citizenship was reported, in the four-year period 1977-78-1980-81, 24.8% were non-Canadian. But there were important regional and linguistic variations. The champions by far were Québec's anglophone universities (McGill, of course, being the largest) where a full 47.1% of full-time appointments

---

[2] P. Fox, *et al.*, *Report of the Committee on Canadian Content*, submitted to the Annual Meeting of the Canadian Political Science Association, Aug. 1973.
[3] T.H.B. Symons, *To Know Ourselves*, AUCC, 1975, Vols. 1 and 2, p. 68.
[4] *Ibid.*
[5] Statistics Canada, *Teachers in Universities*, 1980-81, Ottawa, 1982, Table 2D, pp. 63-64.

went to non-Canadians. By contrast, Québec's francophone universities hired only 11.7% non-Canadians.[6]

Can it be that we are so poor in qualified people that Québec's anglophone universities had to do almost half of their hiring abroad? The Mandel case answers unequivocally: no! A study of hiring in Ontario universities concluded, in fact, that there is discrimination against Canadians in hiring and that were it not for this bias, all Ontario Ph.D.s would be able to find university employment.[7] It is in this light that one should read the statement made to the *Globe and Mail* by Robert Vogel, McGill dean of arts, in relation to the Mandel case: "You have really exceptional students graduating from American universities who are willing to come up and become Canadians... We must do the very best we can do for our students."[8]

On May 7, 1981, in response to the concerns aroused in connection with the Mandel case and others, Lloyd Axworthy, as Minister of Employment and Immigration, announced a new policy to finally impose restrictions on foreign hiring in universities. But judging by McGill, its seems to have made little difference.

In 1980, frustrated by the lack of response from immigration authorities, Mandel wrote to Employment and Immigration Canada:

> Finally, if you are unwilling to do anything about this issue, I would like to suggest in all seriousness that you request the U.S. Department of Immigration to reciprocate. If it were as easy for Canadian academics to get work permits in the U.S. as it is for Americans to get them here, then I might at least have some hope of continuing a career in which I have (foolishly, it now seems) invested so many years of my life.

---

[6] T.H.B. Symons and J.E. Page, *To Know Ourselves*, AUCC, 1984, Vol. 3, pp. 63-64.
[7] L.K. Moffat, *Room at the Bottom: Job Mobility Opportunities for Ontario Academics in the Mid-70's*, Ontario Ministry of Education, 1980, p. 187.
[8] J. McNish, "Immigration Policy Called Risk to Canadian Educators' Jobs", *Globe and Mail,* August 6, 1980, p. 10.

Comparative statistics show that most other countries think it is important that universities hire their own citizens. Most of Canada's imported faculty come from the U.S. and the U.K. Yet in the former only 2% of university staff are not citizens, and in the latter 8%.[9] Obviously, because of its relatively small university system Canada has a special problem. And yet of these three countries, Canada makes it easiest for foreign academics to find university work.

Mandel's fate at McGill demonstrates how "academic freedom" is trotted out to defend what is really academic lawlessness and contempt for the interests of the broader community. It also shows how both the state and CAUT acquiesce in this travesty, making universities a unique institution in our society—not because of their supposed adherence to lofty ideals, for these are more often a smoke screen to conceal the most banal behaviour motivated by ordinary self-interest. They are unique rather for being above the law.

[9] Symons and Page, *To Know Ourselves,* p. 50.

Appendix I

Gibson Committee Proposals Concerning Fair Appointment Practices in Canadian Universities*

Discrimination on non-academic grounds in the making of academic appointments to universities tends to restrict the range of intellectual and ideological resources available within the institutions affected, thereby endangering the academic freedom without which no institution can properly claim to be a university. This threat comes not only from the various forms of discrimination—racial, religious, sexual, and so on—that are proscribed by law in most jurisdictions, but also, perhaps chiefly, from more subtle and insidious forms of prejudice which legal norms are incapable of controlling.

---

* This text, as well as the full Gibson Committee Report, are published in the April 1984 issue of the *CAUT Bulletin*.

It is therefore important that, in addition to complying with every requirement of the law aimed at the elimination of discrimination, universities establish special procedures to ensure that academic appointments at all levels are made on the basis of valid academic criteria. This is not to deny the legitimacy of affirmative action programs designed to favour members of groups that have been historically under-represented on the faculties of Canadian universities. Such measures are intended to remedy the consequences of discriminatory practices and circumstances in the past, and they are to be welcomed if they comply with law and with guidelines of CAUT and other appropriate organizations.

The following guidelines contain CAUT's recommendations for procedures to be established by Canadian universities, together with a description of the circumstances calling for CAUT intervention in cases of alleged discrimination in academic appointments. They are published with the understanding that it is their spirit rather than their precise expression that is important, diversity of approach being a welcome concomitant of academic freedom.

Statements of Criteria

1. Every university department should establish, by methods approved by the university, a priori criteria for academic appointments, including at least:
   (a) the department's overall goals, with special reference to desired areas of specialization within the broader discipline,
   (b) the expectations of the department for its professors, in terms of teaching load, scholarly activities, and university and community service, and
   (c) with respect to each particular appointment, the needs of the department in terms of the areas of teaching and research competence involved, the extent of previous experience desirable, and other factors or characteristics to be taken into account when making the appointment in question.
2. Such criteria should be as precise as possible, and should be made available in advance to all applicants for appointments.

3. No criterion is valid which does not serve one or both of the university's twin goals: the search for knowledge and its dissemination. In particular, it is unacceptable to take account of compatibility, collegiality, religious belief or religious practice, in university appointment criteria. Approved affirmative action programs favouring members of historically under-represented groups should be regarded as serving the university's goals.

Responsibility for Appointment Decisions

4. Every university department should establish, by methods approved by the university, procedures for making academic appointments which clearly delineate the respective functions and responsibilities of all those designated to take part in the appointment process.

5. While the responsibility for academic appointments may appropriately be exercised by either individuals or committees, or by a combination of both, group or shared decision-making carries risk of irresponsibility. Many of the procedural safeguards recommended in these guidelines are intended to provide protection against that risk.

Procedures for Appointments Committees

6. Where appointments committees are established, it is desirable, in the interest of both efficiency and responsibility, that they be relatively small. Nevertheless, unless there are compelling reasons to the contrary, such committees should represent all major constituencies within the department, including the students, and should also have representation from outside the department or the university.

7. Chairpersons of appointments committees should ensure that all members have equal access to all relevant data, as well as adequate opportunity to study it. They should also strive to ensure that full and frank discussion of all relevant issues takes place during committee meetings.

8. Proxy voting should not be permitted in appointments committees.

9. Secret balloting should be permitted whenever there are members of an appointments committee who feel that open voting would be undesirable.

Statements of Reasons

10. The reasons for appointment decisions or advice should be agreed upon (voted upon in the case of committees), recorded, and communicated to the persons adversely affected immediately upon communication of the decisions or advice to higher authority within the university.

11. Reasons given must be precise and related to the previously announced criteria. Any deviations from the criteria must be explained, and must be related to the general goals previously announced.

12. Where reasons for denying an appointment are not given to an unsuccessful candidate, and known facts raise a reasonable inference that improper factors influenced the appointment decision, the university should bear the responsibility of proving that improper factors were not decisive.

Review Procedures

13. The university should provide, in addition to regular "chain of command" confirmation, a fair procedure for reviewing disputed appointment decisions.

14. Re-consideration of disputed decisions by the committee or officers responsible for the original decisions or advice is not a satisfactory review procedure.

15. A review committee, either standing or ad hoc, jointly established by CAUT and the university in question, would be a satisfactory review procedure. Such a committee might also be authorized to review disputed decisions relating to tenure and/or promotion.

16. A satisfactory review mechanism must permit examination of both the procedures employed to reach the disputed decision, and the validity of any allegations that improper factors influenced the decision.

CAUT Intervention

17. Whenever an unsuccessful applicant for an academic appointment at a Canadian university complains that her or his non-appointment was the result of improper discrimination, and the complaint does not appear frivolous or vexatious on its face, CAUT officials may make such informal inquiries about the matter as they deem advisable, and may make such suggestions for a resolution of the dispute as they deem appropriate.

18. If such a dispute remains unresolved, the AF&T Committee, or some other duly authorized body or officer of CAUT, may establish a CAUT Inquiry Committee to investigate the matter in accordance with CAUT procedures, if, after due inquiry, it appears that:

    (a) the charge is not frivolous;

    (b) the charge, while not necessarily proven, is supported by some significant corroborative evidence pointing to at least a plausible suspicion of impropriety; and

    (c) there appears to be no reasonable likelihood that the dispute will be satisfactorily resolved without the establishment of a CAUT Inquiry Committee.

19. Subsequent intervention or action by CAUT should be governed by established CAUT guidelines and procedures.

Appendix II

Canadian Association of University Teachers' Guidelines on Canadianization and the University

Preamble

One function among the many legitimately assigned to a university is to develop an awareness and understanding of the society in which we live. This society, of course, has local and national as well as international aspects, all of which require attention. The university thus has an important role to play in the development of community and national identities. If we assume that university faculty play an important or even dominant role in the learning process, then we can properly expect that faculty members at Canadian universities be familiar with the Canadian situation and, further, be committed to the development and enrichment of the Canadian community, or engage themselves to acquire this familiarity and commitment.

The Canadian university community must also be concerned that qualified Canadians be given opportunities for employment at Canadian universities.

The C.A.U.T. is opposed to the use of the authority of governments and legislatures to enforce or encourage rules concerning methods of appointments within universities. If this position is to be maintained, the following conditions are necessary.

1. openings available at Canadian universities should be made known to Canadians by means of advertisements in the *C.A.U.T. Bulletin* and *University Affairs* and by formal and informal employment services, including departments of manpower or labour. Such searches must not be avoided or their purpose defeated by appointments made on the basis of personal contacts only;
2. the appointment of a person who is not a Canadian or legally a resident of Canada should be justified to the satisfaction of a university or faculty committee.

The C.A.U.T. further urges that academic, professional, and government agencies co-operate in the preparation, publication, and annual revision of five- to ten-year projections of positions available and of graduate degrees granted in each academic discipline at Canadian universities. These projections would allow individual students a better opportunity to plan further careers, and universities a better opportunity to encourage Canadian talents in areas of projected needs through the development of adequate graduate programmes in those areas.

The C.A.U.T. is always prepared to investigate any allegations of anti-Canadian discrimination in appointments, and to endeavour to correct improper or unsatisfactory practices.

Guidelines

1. For the purpose of these guidelines, a person who, on the date of application for a university post, is a landed immigrant or holds a ministerial permit as a consequence of being a refugee or of being prohibited from applying for landed immigrant status should not be distinguished from Canadian applicants.

2. For each position a set of qualifications relevant to that opening and the relative importance of each should be clearly stated. These qualifications should not place graduates of Canadian programmes or Canadian graduates of programmes at home or abroad at an unfair disadvantage.

3. The opening and the required qualifications should be called to the attention of Canadian applicants by appropriate procedures such as wide advertisement, letters to Canadian universities, etc. That is, there should be active search for qualified Canadian candidates.

4. Each university with a bi-cameral system of government should establish a university-wide appointments review committee, where one does not already exist. In any case, the following would be desirable arrangements for such a committee.

    i. The committee should be elected by a senior academic body or other appropriate body and should have a clear majority of full-time faculty members on it;

    ii. The committee should, in the first instance, advise the president on all appointments;

    iii. The committee should also supply the senior academic body annually with a list of appointments made as well as its decisions as to whether each was adequately advertised in Canada;

    iv. A representative of the faculty association should sit on the committee as a non-voting participant;

    v. Before recommending any new appointments, this body should, *inter alia*, ensure that these guidelines are adhered to. In particular it should assure itself that:

       (a) The qualifications listed were reasonable and the selection procedures fair;

       (b) An active effort was made to recruit Canadians.

    The department seeking to make an appointment of a non-Canadian should be charged with making the case for the appointment to the satisfaction of this body.

5. Each university with a uni-cameral system of government should strike an appointments committee at the faculty rather

than the university level. In other respects, the recommendations of item 4, above, should be followed, *mutatis mutandis*.

6. The appointments should be offered to the best-qualified Canadian, who meets the stated requirements, unless the university-wide review committee, or if it does not exist, the senior academic body, is persuaded that the appointment in the case of a non-Canadian is justified.

7. Once appointed, the nationality of the faculty member should not affect the terms and conditions of that employment. These include, for example, academic freedom, salary, promotion, and tenure.

Council Resolution (1977)

2ND REVISED EDITION

TURNING THE TIDE

The U.S. and Latin America
by Noam Chomsky

Regarding U.S. policy in Latin America, *Turning the Tide* succinctly provides the most cogent available descriptions of what is going on, and why. It will be a central tool for everyone who wants to promote peace and justice in the Americas.

Noam Chomsky reveals the aim and impact of U.S. policy in Latin America by examining the historical record and current events. With this as backdrop, he also shows the connection between Latin American policy and broader nuclear and international politics and explains the logic and role of the Cold War for both super-powers. Finally, Chomsky looks at why we accept Reaganesque rhetoric in light of the role of the media and the intelligentsia in the numbing of our awareness. He concludes by describing what we can do to resist.

Turning the Tide is a succinct volume ideal for understanding the broad factors governing U.S. policy in Latin America, the role of the Cold War, and the role of the media and intellectuals with respect to each.

Noam Chomsky is professor of Linguistics and Philosophy and Institute Professor at M.I.T.; recipient of honorary degrees from the University of London, University of Chicago, Delhi University, and four other colleges and universities; fellow of the American Academy of Arts and Sciences, member of the National Academy of Arts and Sciences, and member of the National Academy of Sciences; author of numerous books and articles on linguistics, philosophy, intellectual history and contemporary issues.

Paperback ISBN: 0-920057-78-0   **$14.95**
Hardcover ISBN: 0-920057-76-4   **$29.95**

THE COMING OF WORLD WAR THREE

Volume 1
From Protest to Resistance / the International War System

Dimitrios I. Roussopoulos

This book is **not** about the arms race, it is about the peace movement. In presenting an analysis of the strengths and weaknesses of actions for peace, Dimitrios Roussopoulos shows us what we must really do to prevent a third world war.

ISBN: 0-920057-02-0 $14.95

BLACK ROSE BOOKS

Write for free catalogue of more than 110 books:

Black Rose Books
3981, boul. St. Laurent
Montréal, Québec
H2W 1Y5

Printed by
the workers of
Ateliers Graphiques Marc Veilleux Inc.
Cap-Saint-Ignace, Qué.
for
Black Rose Books Ltd.